SALMON & SEA TROUT FISHING

Charles Bingham

SALMON & SEA TROUT FISHING

B T Batsford Ltd, London

'To Pamela'

ISBN 0 7134 5639 6 (cased)

Typeset by Lasertext Ltd
and printed in Great Britain by
Oxford University Press
Printing House
for the publishers
B. T. Batsford Ltd.
4 Fitzhardinge Street
London W1H 0AH

Contents

II SEA TROUT

Foreword

When a new fishing book is written it seems that the author or his publishers must justify it in some way. This may lead to a gimmicky approach, or hollow claims to total originality. Charles Bingham prefers commonsense, and neither of the two faults I have mentioned are to be found in this book. And yet the originality, as modestly offered as anybody who knows Charles would expect, is there for all to see.

A few years ago now Charles approached me, in my role as Editor of *Countrysport*, to ask if I would be prepared to consider a series of articles on fishing in the West Country. Initially, I accepted them for no other reason than that they were well written and, possibly more than that, they kept me in touch with that delightful part of the world. I had lived just over the border in Cornwall for a number of years and, although I was by then living in the Scottish Highlands, I enjoyed the opportunity to return to the intimate scenery of the South West. For a few brief moments, I would slip away from the high mountains and glens, the deer forests and grouse moors, and return with nostalgia to the soft combes and mysterious tors. I pictured the peaceful country, the flight of the woodcock from carefully prepared coverts; above all, I pictured the tree-clad streams where silver-flanked salmon renewed the cycle of life and death and wild sea trout swirled in the pool tails at dusk.

And then I began to see something more in Charles's writing. I might not agree with everything that he says, but my experience is different to his. I was raised, in terms of salmon and sea trout, on the mighty rivers of the North, and this profoundly affected my thinking on fish and fishing. Charles also fishes these waters but, with his varied experience on waters in Hampshire and the West Country, he brings a fresh and enquiring mind to the search for solutions to the problems that they pose for the fisherman, keen for success. Whether he is fishing his home waters or tempting sea trout on Loch Maree, there is originality in his approach and conclusions, and this book shows that this quality has been present since the day he caught his first salmon, so many years ago.

Salmon and sea trout are quite wonderful creatures, offering a host of questions to be answered. Any writer who sets out to describe the methods of their capture, the when, where, what and how of the sport, has to admit that the fundamental question of 'why' eludes us all. Nobody can state, hand on heart, that he knows the exact reason why a salmon or sea trout is ever tempted to take a whirr of metal or an intricate tying of feather, fur and silk into its mouth. The tyro fisherman is therefore well advised to rely heavily on the advice and experience of those who have trod the river bank before.

We all have our theories and hypotheses, some more likely than others. What Charles shows is that, since his early days, he has had the ability to learn quickly with the intelligence and thoughtfulness to accept, reject or adapt what has been presented as knowledge. And he has had plenty of opportunity to put theory into practice. His dedication has led him to make his career, for many years, in teaching others to fish. While many sit at their desks and dream, Charles is casting a line over his beloved waters. And so, you see, he already has behind him the experience that most others would take a lifetime to achieve.

This book, which is truly written, makes a significant contribution to our thoughts on salmon and sea trout. It offers sound advice on tackle and technique, and it is tempered with recollections of the author's experiences, for must not every good book entertain as well as instruct?

I feel honoured to have been asked to write the foreword to Charles's book, and seize the opportunity to thank him publicly for the pleasure that I have gained from his writing.

Crawford Little

Acknowledgements

All black and white photographs by Charles and Pamela Bingham with the following exceptions: David Jenkins of Bourton-on-the-Water, figure 5; Caroline Frost of Boston, America, figures 93–97; 20th Earl of Moray, Darnaway Castle, Morayshire, figure 98; Tony Allen, Little Testwood, Hampshire, figures 101, 103, 104, 109, 117, 118; David Uren, Tenterden, Kent, figure 115; Dr Mark Stapleton, London, figures 121 and 122; Lara Bingham, Devonshire, figure 126.

I would like to thank the following people for taking colour photographs: (jacket) Philip Massey; (colour plates 5, 6, 7 and 9) Tony Allen; (colour plate 8) Lindsay Parker.

I especially wish to acknowledge the help of Tony Allen — a great angler and staunch friend. He has read and corrected the manuscript, supplied photographs, assisted with drawings and given encouragement.

Introduction

There is a lake in Shropshire which is fed by a stream running from a spring; the spring bubbles out of the ground into an overflowing stone trough. Attached to the trough by a chain is a brass drinking bell for thirsty golfers from the nearby course. As a child of 7 years I caught fresh water shrimps in the bell and was shouted at by the golfers for making the water muddy by my shrimp catching. The following year I graduated to the lake; this held many striped and spiny perch, which I went after with a red float, a wriggling worm and my grandfather. From then until present middle age the wild and lonely places — meadows, moorlands, forests and the rivers and lakes — have beckoned and held me. The pursuit of fish has been at the spine of it all, with the manner of their taking and the beauty of the surroundings of more importance than numbers on the bank, though that concerned me too.

As a schoolboy I plopped my bushy fly from behind a shielding tree trunk onto portly cruising chub — and in excitement struck too soon before the thick white lips closed on the feathery lure I had purchased from the village ironmonger in a packet labelled 'Chub Flies'. In season I used a struggling grasshopper. When fly-casting I cracked off minute black gnats on the back cast, when in pursuit of dace, which I then cooked and ate in two bony mouthfuls. No one taught me how to cast. The teeth of pike rasped my tender eager fingers when I caught them spinning, using the bottom section of a broken fly-rod and a homemade, treble-hooked spoon that I had cut and hammered into shape with finger-blistered persistence from a sheet of copper.

Trout, brownies only in those days, became the prey after my school years, and salmon, which followed, became my fishing passion. Sea trout too — at night under the myriad stars and the lonely silver moon, which shines down over Devon onto my solitary figure wading in the dark sliding water.

I have never ceased to learn from others, for no matter how far our search for fishing truths has taken us, there is always someone who has acquired a facet of knowledge beyond our own experience. The technical competence and water wisdom have been gained slowly over many years. In teaching others to fish three or four days a week for seven months in the year I have had the good fortune to spend more time than most beside a beginner with a rod in his hand. There is today a great shortage of time in which to learn a new activity, and the demands of work and home life absorb much of our daily lives. In this book, as in my working life as owner of a game-fishing school, I will do my best to shorten the time you spend finding out. I will also try to bring you the sound of the running rivers and the touch of raindrops on your hands.

Glossary of angling terms

Adipose fin – small fin on the back of a game fish between the dorsal fin and the tail

AFTM scale – defines the weight of a fly-line

Alevin – the minute fish which hatches from an ova

Backing – an additional length of strong, thin line joined to, and beneath, the fly-line on a reel

Backing up – a method of fishing the fly whilst moving from the tail to the head of the pool

Baggot – a salmon swollen with eggs which it has been unable to extrude

Bail arm – that part of a fixed spool reel which gathers and winds the line on to the pool

Bank – (in boat fishing) an area of shallow water in a loch

Bass – a bag made of woven raffia for holding and transporting fish

Blow line – (also known as floss line) undressed fluffy line blown out by the wind to carry the fly away from the boat when dapping

Bob fly – the fly closest to the butt of the leader, and thus the fly-line, when a team of flies is being fished

Burn – a small Scottish stream

Butt – (of leader) the thickest part of a tapered leader where it joins the fly-line

Butt – (of rod) the handle end of a rod

Dangle – (on the) position of fly, or taking fish, when straight downstream of the angler

Dropper – a second or third fly fished on a leader between the point and bob flies

Dubbing needle – a pointed, fly-dressing tool

Finnock – a small Scottish sea trout

Fish – the term usually refers to a salmon rather than a trout or sea trout

Flopy – a rubber plug bait from France

Fry – a small young fish (after the alevin stage)

Gaff – a pointed hook on a shaft for landing fish

Gape – defines the gap measurement between the point and shank of a hook

Gillie – person who should have detailed knowledge of a river and is employed to assist an angler

Gravid – (hen) fish with well-developed roe, sometimes dripping from the vent

Groyne – man-made protrusion from river bank to create a salmon lie

Hopper – term used by West Country salmon netsman to define a grilse

Kelt – spawned salmon or sea trout

Kype – upward hook on lower jaw of cock fish

Leader – (cast) the length of nylon (used to be gut) joining the fly line to the tail (point) fly

Ledger – see Paternoster

Lie – a favoured place where fish rest in a river

Lure – wide term embracing spinning baits, artificial flies, plugs and so on

Mend – to move the fly-line on the water, after the initial cast, by switching upstream or downstream to decrease or increase the speed of passage of a fly across the river to the angler's bank

Mepps – a revolving spoon bait

Nymph – (natural and artificial) underwater stage in life cycle of some insects

'On the fin' – a term describing a feeding river trout which has taken up a position close to the water surface from which it may readily take passing floating natural flies

Otter – a device to release spinning baits caught on the river bed

Parr – a small salmon or sea trout, only a few inches in length, in the early river stage of life cycle

Paternoster – (ledger) method of fishing a spinning bait, worm or prawn slowly and close to the river bed (see fig. 108)

Peal West Country term for a sea trout of any size

Peal sling – a quick-release harness, generally of leather, by which a Gye net is carried on the angler's back

Plug – an artificial vaned bait, usually fish-shaped, sometimes jointed, which darts, dives, rises and pops about underwater when retrieved by a spinning reel

Point fly – the fly at the end of a leader

Rapala – a type of plug bait

Redd – depression cut in gravel by fish in river bed in which female deposits ova and where ova are fertilized by milt of cock fish

Run-off – the downstream, tail end of a river pool

School peal – small sea trout in a shoal on first return to river in summer from the sea

Scissors – (to be hooked in the) description of the point of the angle between the upper and lower jaws of a fish

Sea lice – a suckered louse found on flanks and back of salmon and sea trout when they enter the river from the sea. Denotes a very fresh fish as they drop off after two or three days in fresh water

Sea trout – a migratory brown trout

Sewin – a Welsh term for a sea trout

Shooting head – first 10 yd of a tapered fly-line that is cut off and needle knotted to special monofilament backing. Enables long casts to be 'shot'.

Skate – (skid) a fly crossing the river, or drawn over the loch surface, on top of, or in, the water surface film

Sliced hook – type of hook with barbed shank used in worm fishing

Smolt – an immature salmon or sea trout migrating down river in spring (usually April or May) to make first entry to the sea

Spate – the rise and fall of the water level in a river following rain in the catchment area

Spigot bobbin holder – a fly dressing tool that holds a reel of silk

Split cane – a rod of hexagon cross section formed of six faced strips of cane bonded, or silk wrapped, together

Spoon – a type of spinning bait

Stale fish – a salmon or sea trout which has been in fresh water for some months. The term is most frequently used in autumn and is likely to denote a dark or red fish

Stickle – a shallow section of river between two pools

Tail fly – see point fly

Toby – a type of spinning bait

Trace – a short length, usually about

one metre, of nylon between the swivel at the end of a spinning line and the bait

UDN – ulcerative dermal necrosis - a fish disease

Walking up – a method of persuading a hooked salmon to move upstream

Weight forward line – a fly-line tapered only at the front end where the weight is concentrated. The greater length of the line is of small diameter to facilitate 'shooting' and thus distance casting

Wye weight – see figure 10

Wind knot – a knot formed unintentionally in the leader whilst casting. Weakens the leader.

I
SALMON

1 Knowledge of the fish

Spawning

After working in my study all morning it was a relief to put on gum boots, a waxed jacket, whistle up the dog Ben, and thumb-stick in hand make my way down the hill to the river Lyd. Hanging over the old stone bridge, which had been built long before the first motor car, I looked down at the river through polarized glasses. It was the end of the first week in December, and because there had been little rain for several days, I could see the gravel stream-bed through water of almost absolute clarity. I decided to wander down the waterway to look for otter tracks on the sandy banks, watch the dippers, and look out for kingfishers.

The river is barely 20 ft wide at this point, and the shallowness enabled me to cross and re-cross whilst Ben splashed to one side and behind. I was also on the lookout for salmon, for the Lyd is a prolific spawning tributary of the Tamar, and many grilse and two sea-winter fish cut their redds in the gravel at the end of November and in December in our isolated valley. I walked on along the grassy bank beneath a willow tree which hangs over a deep pool where children from a nearby farm swim noisily in summer

1 *A salmon spawning site. A vertical stick marks the site where salmon dig their redds in the gravel of this moorland stream. (This is the actual footbridge in The Torn Gill Flap Story, chapter 14.)*

The tail of this pool shallows and widens into a splay of gravel.

As I walked, immersed in thoughts, I was startled by a momentary bulge in the water as a salmon, disturbed by my sudden appearance, fled to hide under the far bank. There were two of them, no doubt a cock and a hen, and the redd she had cut in the gravel was clearly visible as a bank of piled up small stones of lighter colour than the surrounding area. And that is where it all begins, the salmon story, in gravel redds, in the headwaters of their rivers. The next morning she had gone, having smoothed the redd, perhaps helped in the levelling by the current; but in the tiny stones below the surface would be one or two thousand eggs. Being a hen fish of 8-9 lb she might extrude six thousand ova—but not all in one place. No doubt she had moved elsewhere to repeat her actions, cutting another redd or two to spread the chances of survival for her offspring.

Juvenile river life

I would like to say that I saw those newly-hatched alevins three months later, but this was not so; the water was high in late spring, and alevins are very small indeed, having a yolk sac beneath their bodies to sustain them for the first month. When this sac has been absorbed, they become free-feeding, and are known as fry; and then, without definition in time, they are called parr when they have grown to 3–4 in. in length. Parr live and feed in the same manner as wild brown trout and will be caught unintentionally on wet and dry flies by trout fishers. They must be returned to the water, and the angler should do this with care, touching them as little as possible.

Try to do this under water, but if they have to be handled, wet and cool your hand for some moments in the river

2a Above — *salmon parr (5 in.). Streamlined body, distinctly forked tail. Well-defined finger marks on flanks. Below — brown trout (6 in.). Thick body, shallow forked tail. Red or brown adipose fin. White line on leading edge of lower fins.*

2b *An April salmon smolt. Size may be gauged from No. 2 long mepps which it has taken. Fish returned alive.*

before touching one. Parr may be distinguished from brown trout by their adipose fin, which is clear in colour like the other fins; the trout's adipose is red or orange and the leading edge of the anal fin is white. Parr are more stream-lined, silvery and have many distinct grey bars or finger marks on their flanks and a well-forked tail.

Although there may be some variation in the number of years parr spend in the river, before becoming silver in colour and as smolts (6 in. long) migrating down to the sea in March or April, the average period is two years. During this time I am certain the parr move down the river valley steadily towards the sea because I have caught many some miles below the spawning beds when trout fishing, whilst I have not been troubled by a great number in the area of the original redds. Smolts on their seaward migration downriver to

the estuary in spring have a voracious appetite: when they attempt to take salmon spinning baits of 2 in. in length the treble hook becomes jammed in the mouth, and it is very difficult to unhook and release them. Once again if you do this, wet your hands first.

The marine period

In the sea the smolts feed greedily, putting on weight rapidly before returning to the parent river to spawn. How they find their way in the North Atlantic is not known but they are able to identify their own river on the coast by their sense of smell on their return. The time spent at sea varies. The first to come back are the one sea winter fish or grilse, which weigh in the region of 5 lb although this will vary from 4 lb to as much as 7, 8 or 9 lb. The grilse start to enter the river from the sea in July and continue into the autumn, having spent 15 or 16 months in salt water. Other salmon spend two, three or more winters at sea and may enter the river at any

3a *Top 20 lb hen salmon. Caught March. Scale examination in laboratory showed that the fish had spent two years in the river and three years in the sea; it had not spawned. (See letter from South West Water.)*

3b *A kelt. Note over-large head, and back parallel to line of belly compared with the curved lines of the fresh hen fish in fig. 3a. This kelt was returned alive - note eye looking down; eye of dead fish looks out at right angles to the body.*

time of the year, although some months are more favoured than others. In general, autumn entries have increased at the expense of the spring runs in the last 20 years but this may be cyclical. I recall two schoolboy brothers who took in the region of one hundred salmon from the Findhorn one April in the early 1950s; such an achievement would be unlikely today. On some rivers there is a heavy entry of fresh fish as late as the second half of November and into December.

The river and sea life of a returned salmon may be ascertained if scales are taken from the flank of the fish for examination under a microscope. Beside my desk is a photograph of a 20 lb hen fish caught in March 1981. I had removed half a dozen scales for examination by South West Water, who wrote:

> *Dear Charles,*
>   *The scales indicated that the fish had spent three winters at sea, plus two in the river before migrating. There were no spawning marks.*
>   *Best wishes,*
>   *Peter*

The migration months

You must enquire the timing of the returning runs of salmon into any particular river, or a long journey to take a fishing holiday may be wasted. I remember a pupil coming in the early spring to Devon for instruction in fishing the fly, having booked a salmon holiday on the Island of Mull in May. Having fished the Lussa on that island in July for a couple of weeks in two consecutive seasons and read the lodge fishing book, I warned him that very few

4   *A salmon leaping Tavistock weir on river Tavy in October whilst making its way upstream in a flood to spawn in the headwaters in December.*

5 *The 'running mark'—a pink circle about 1 in. across where skin on the belly of this salmon has been worn by river bed abrasion in the up-river journey.*

6 *The weir across the river Tavy in Tavistock with the fish pass on the left. This pass is used in small spates when insufficient water runs over the weir.*

7a *The 'kype'. The hooked jaw of a July cock salmon, Black Dart tube fly visible in the jaw. A hen fish does not have a kype.*

7b *Badgers eat dead salmon kelts. Note prominent claw marks of tracks on river-side sand.*

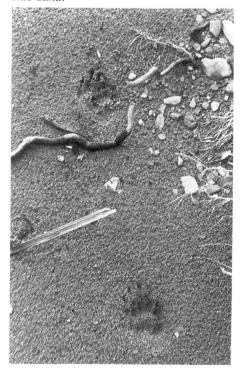

fish entered earlier than the beginning of that month. In my home area, South West Water compile an annual report on their rivers, listing not only the total salmon and sea trout catch for the season but the monthly results. It takes little thought on the part of an angler with a 1 in:mile map to calculate that if a river shows 30 fish for March they are likely to be taken in the first few miles above the sea. Staying at a hotel with fishing 30 miles upstream is unlikely to be fruitful at that time for the salmon will not have reached their beats. On the other hand, such a hotel should be considered later in the year when the lower beats may not yield much—the salmon running straight through on each lifting of the river level following rainfall.

The spawned fish or kelt

It is interesting to understand the progress, or rather the death, of the original parent fish, which after spawning are known as kelts. Three weeks after my Lyd walk, just before Christmas, Ben and I made an excursion up a tributary of the Dart high on the moor. Spawning was over, the eggs secure beneath the gravel, but it was saddening to count the many dead salmon rotting on the river bed. They had given their all and then died of exhaustion after completing the life cycle, and their bodies had become food for foxes, badgers trundling along the river bank at night, ravens and carrion crows.

Some kelts do not die but swim down river to the sea to feed and recover; they re-enter the river after a year or two to spawn a second time. Very few succeed for of the salmon passing up a river to spawn, only four or five per cent are on a second visit. But kelts must be given their chance by being returned to the river if caught whilst you fish for springers in February and March.

The latest I caught a kelt was in April. They may be recognized by the line of the belly and back being parallel, whilst on a 'clean fish' the belly and back are convex to each other. Before you have seen the fish you will have a good idea that you have one on as they have little stamina in the fight. Kelts look thin and have heads that appear over-large; they may be a deceptive bright silver colour.

The reduction in body weight of salmon during river life will be discussed later, but a fish entering a river in March at 10 lb weight may have been reduced to 6 lb the following March as a kelt after spawning.

In the early weeks of the season you can very occasionally catch a baggot or rawner. This is a salmon which has attempted to spawn, but for some reason has failed to eject the eggs it holds. The latest I have caught such a fish in the headwaters of a river was on 17 April when I landed and returned a hen of 15 lb, which took a No. 4 Thunder & Lightning fly. It was an unsightly shade of green and had a swollen belly.

Parasites and diseases

A salmon caught within two or three days of entering the river may have sea lice (*Lepeophtheirus salmonis*) on the back, flanks and in the area of the anal fin; such a fish is a highly desirable catch because the lice are an indication that it is fresh run from the sea and that the flesh will be of the highest quality.

Small pale-coloured gill maggots (*Salmincola salmonea*) will often be seen on a salmon, moving about on the gills if the gill flaps are lifted. The maggots are said to indicate that a fish is a kelt, but this is not a reliable guide as I have often caught salmon in May and June some miles above the sea that were heavily infested with these parasites.

Ulcerative dermal necrosis (UDN) causes a breakdown of the skin of the salmon and usually shows first on the head or nose, followed by patches on the body. These patches may turn white from the initial pink as fungi invade the infected area. Diseased fish usually move to the quieter sides of the river and may rest not far below the surface. From my own observations I believe that a higher percentage die than recover, but there is no doubt that the lesions heal in some cases because mended, slightly depressed places will at times be found

8a *Tracks of a mink. They attack salmon at the parr stage.*

8b *Mink traps are dug into the river bank just above water level and baited with a fish head.*

8c *Mink and folding .410 shot gun.*

9 *These salmon have UDN and will probably die. Diseased salmon are usually found in the quiet shallow sides of a river out of the main current.*

on fish caught in the upper reaches of a river. The new dark skin covering the formerly diseased areas is tender and readily breaks under a blow of the priest. The disease appears to be reducing on many rivers after being prevalent for several years.

Conserving energy and choice of lies

From the time a salmon enters a river until it returns once more to the ocean as a kelt after spawning, it does not feed. It is true that salmon may be caught on a worm or prawn but they are still not *feeding*. If a river holds, for example, two thousand salmon by August, it would take an immense army of worms drifting down the river to satisfy them— such supplies do not exist, as anyone who has tried to find a worm at short notice will agree; and there are no prawns at all. I personally clean all the

10 *left   Tracks of an otter. Otters will kill salmon but protected and insufficiently common on most rivers to be a serious detrimental factor.*

salmon we catch and have yet to find one with a stomach that is anything other than a white empty gut. The fish's source of energy is thus its own body, the fat of which will be partially absorbed to provide the power needed to propel it from the estuary to the spawning redds. Body weight will also be transferred to the two developing sacs of eggs, which in a 10 lb fish on entry from the sea in March might each be 4 in. long and $\frac{1}{2}$ in. in diameter. By November each sac will have expanded to 8–9 in. in length and 2 in. in diameter and will fill the body cavity—the walls of which will have become thin in the reduced state of the salmon.

These demands upon the fish's energy store are such that the salmon conserves

its resources and will find resting places, or lies as they are called, where energy expenditure is at a minimum. Simultaneously, the lie must provide safety and the water flow a sufficient supply of oxygen. These places are not difficult to pick out as you are walking up a beat - especially upstream. The lies are occupied or vacated as the river rises or falls because the salmon likes to have at least 4 ft of water over his back. The most favoured lie is in front of a rock, boulder or slab of concrete placed on the bottom; ahead of a weed bed; or just before a sand bank shelves up at the tail of a pool. The lie is not generally *behind* such obstructions, although it may be alongside, or a little off and below, a man-made groyne.

An understanding of the movement of salmon from one lie to another as the river rises and falls is vital to success, because it is no use fishing lies that have

11 *Salmon travel up fish ladders and may then be caught as they pause to rest above the weir.*

12 *Salmon like to have an obstruction to their rear; they will lie in front of weirs in high water and below weirs in low water where cover is produced by turbulence*

just been vacated or others not yet occupied owing to unsuitable water depths or flows. Detailed knowledge of the lies in a river will only be gained over a number of seasons, which is the main reason why an angler should persist at one water rather than try to learn the secrets of many. In time the places to fish at certain water heights can be established on arrival at the river by a single glance at the level in relation to some fixed object. On one river I go at once to look at a rock with a light-coloured top—if this rock is not submerged I return to the car and drive home because the river is too low. If the top is submerged by a depth of one dipped finger-joint, or two or three, or the water comes up to my wrist, I know

the pools and lies to visit. This depth together with the clarity and temperature of the water also govern the size of the fly I choose, as will be discussed later.

It is not often that I make a wasted journey, finding the rock top clear of the water, for at my home I place a dustbin lid upside down in the garden.

13 *The deep head of this pool is at A, with the shallow tail or run-off at B. In high water salmon lie in front of the rocks at C. As a spate recedes, fish move into trough D (which is a depression in the river bed). A further reduction in water volume will cause them to swim forward again to rest in front of the rocks at E. Finally, as the water level drops to low they take refuge in the deep turbulent throat at F where they are protected from above by bushes. At F they await the next spate, perhaps staying there for some weeks if there is no rain.*

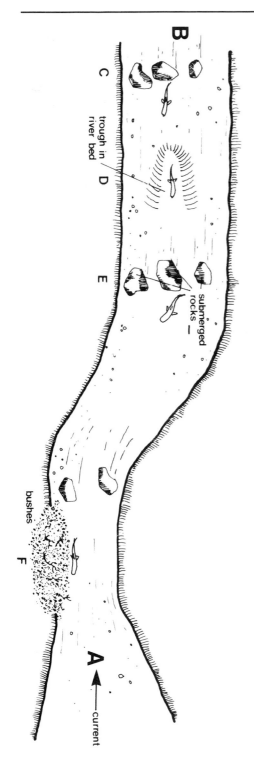

If this permanent rain gauge is filled with water after a wet day or night I know a visit to the river is likely to be worth while.

Water temperature and volume

Cold water

Let us consider a river where the salmon season opens on 1 February. The demand for water by vegetation and trees is minimal in the winter, whilst rainfall should be sufficient to saturate the chalk aquiffer from which the springs arise to feed the southern salmon rivers—Hampshire Avon, Test and Itchen. The great mass of peat on the moors of the north and west will become sodden to feed those rivers running down from the hills; reservoirs will have filled and the heavier agricultural land may be unworkable owing to surface water. Rivers will be above that level that is likely to prevail throughout the summer, other than in times of spate.

It seems logical that salmon would run upstream under these conditions, but although they may enter the lower reaches their progress is slow; instead of being governed by the volume of water they are held back by the river temperature. Salmon do not like to run in cold water and are reluctant to ascend white water (weirs and fish ladders) if the temperature is below about 40°F. In cold waters the fish are lethargic.

The opening week on a river will usually see a few salmon landed as there will have been a trickle of entrants throughout December and January, and the rods may 'mop up' these early or late arrivals, which may be described as 'creepers'. (If the river opens on 1 January, some of these salmon may be winter fish which had intended to spawn in the lower reaches of the river in that month, or perhaps February, if there is a gravel bed available.) If a freeze up follows the opening week the temperature and volume will fall and all movement upstream, or into the river from the estuary, will cease.

In March a water temperature of perhaps 45°F may be expected, and the first substantial run of fish on a spring river will enter if the water is at a good level. The fish, however, will still be relatively inactive, hugging the bottom, jumping infrequently and showing so rarely that the angler may mistakenly imagine the river to be empty. I remember asking a frogman in March to tell me the population of a pool that for days had shown no sign of salmon occupation—he reported fish, in no great numbers it was true, but they were there, on the bottom. Thus, at this time of the year, you must fish deep.

It has become fashionable to advocate fly-fishing at all times, and whilst I am one of the first to embrace this most pleasurable method, it is not the most effective in the early months when you must go down to the fish. Instead it is best to spin, if the rules of the river so allow. Success at this time of year follows the gaining of a detailed knowledge of the contours of the river bed. Once the angler knows these ups and downs he can weight his minnow, and alter the speed of retrieve to ensure that the bait fishes close to the bottom.

Warm water

At the end of April and in early May the water level is likely to drop and the temperature rise to 48°F and above.

Salmon show more frequently and run upstream to enter the middle beats; the angler may fish closer to the surface because salmon will rise to take a fly—and a fly it should be for both results and pleasure.

In my opinion the salmon has a built-in calendar of the months to go before spawning. Whilst a few will reach the upper river by May and June most take their time, moving up from pool to pool as water levels allow. If a drought of three or four months interrupts their progress they will take full advantage of the ensuing spate to run many miles in one go, once again catching up with their calendar. Grilse tend to run faster through the lower river. It is not uncommon to see three or four silver fish jump in a forward-arching manner and then to see them again 40 yd upstream three or four minutes later. This is probably because a fish entering in summer or autumn must pursue a more rapid schedule if it is to arrive at the spawning beds at the same time as earlier entrants. At the end of the summer drought of 1984 a heavy spate in the third week of September gave fish that had been waiting in the estuary the chance to dash upstream. A friend watching Kilbury Weir on the lower Dart counted salmon and grilse going over at the rate of one a minute.

As the water cools once more in autumn and the volume increases after the equinoctial gales, the spinning rod and the fly fished on a sinking line may once more be used. I usually continue to use a floating line throughout October, only taking up the spinning rod if the river becomes really high.

2 Landing equipment

Hooking and playing salmon will be discussed under the various fishing method headings. Landing is considered in advance as the equipment is common to fly, spinning and bait fishing.

The hand and beaching

To obtain the fullest satisfaction from salmon fishing go to the river with a fly-rod, a spool of nylon of adequate strength, half a dozen flies in a battered leather wallet and no landing equipment at all. There is a primaeval feeling when one stands up to the thighs in a river playing a fish with nothing to land him with other than your wits, the beach (if any) and one free hand. This situation sharpens the reactions and develops the resources—and when it is all accomplished and you look down at the gleaming bar of silver on the grass or gravel you'll feel better than you've ever felt before. I don't suggest that you adopt this approach to start with—there are other, more certain ways—but let it be an aim to be achieved on a river after you have safely landed several fish in your career. It will then become an indulgence in suitable circumstances or a reserve in an emergency.

The ring formed by thumb and index finger is immensely powerful, being capable of gripping and lifting at the wrist of the tail a two or three sea-winter salmon up to 20 lb. I cannot claim experience with the hand beyond that weight. If you are standing in the river without a suitable place for bleaching, the fish must be lifted with the palm of the hand towards the head to clear it from the water as you step up onto the bank. If a gently sloping shore is available the fish may be beached, pushed from behind further up the sand, gravel or mud with the palm of the hand toward the tail, the wrist of which is then gripped to carry the salmon away from the river to a safe place. Wipe your hand over mud or sand in advance to get a better grip.

The actual beaching is not difficult to accomplish—play out the fish until well-tired, swim him towards the bank head-first and at right angles, then continue to draw him ashore by rod pressure as you nip between him and the river and push the prize up the bank before lifting. A grilse may be beached but not tailed, for this slim, athletic 'one sea-winter' fish has no knuckle to the tail to afford a grip.

'Get your fingers under his gill flaps' is well-meant advice when one is dealing with a squirming thrashing salmon; but it is not particularly practical owing to the difficulty that will be experienced in lifting the slippery gill flaps. If a grip on the head is desired it is much better to

14a   *A two sea-winter salmon may be tailed ....*

14b   *with the hand facing up or down.*

span the skull from above and press in the gill flaps with the thumb on one side and the fingers on the other; the flaps will collapse inwards and a good hold may be obtained under the bones of the skull. When salmon fishing I usually take a net, but if I don't have it I'm not bothered—I always have my hand and the added enjoyment of a greater challenge in the landing.

The tailer

I have placed this piece of equipment after the hand for it is by no means unusual to commence a landing with a tailer and, following one or two efforts, throw the gadget ashore in disgust before settling the matter by hand tailing. Without doubt more fish are lost with tailers than with any other method, but they are used for a number of

15 *When a salmon has been beached it may be pushed ashore and lifted.*

16 *A grilse has too slim a tail to be lifted. It may be held and brought ashore by pressing in the gill covers.*

reasons. The bye-laws on a river may require an angler to return fish that are described as unclean: these include kelts, heavily gravid hens (identified by their swollen belly and an occasional egg emerging from the vent), and cock fish, from which the white milt runs freely when lifted from the water. As a tailer will enable you to land such a salmon undamaged the device may be carried legally at all times.

The tailer consists of a hollow metal tube 2 ft 6 in. in length with a hand grip and leather wrist-strap at one end. From the other end is drawn out a thick, twisted wire cable, 2 ft 3 in. in length, and a very thin twisted wire, 1 ft long attached to the end of it. At the end of this wire is a brass ring that slides up and down the cable. The tailer is set up by drawing the brass ring up the thick

17   *Tailer set for use. Leather strap encloses wrist to ensure the tailer is not pulled out of the grip by a heavy salmon.*

18   *(Left) A safe way to carry the tailer.*

cable to the place where it enters the hollow tube. A D-shaped ring is thus formed, which is slipped over the tail of the salmon and moved forwards to the rear of the dorsal fin. A sharp pull will cause the thin wire noose and brass ring to slide down the tapering body of the fish and tighten around the wrist of the tail. The fish may then be lifted from the water. At the base of the tail of a two or three sea-winter salmon are two knobs of gristle, which enable the noose to take a good grip. A grilse does not have these knobs and, being without such a knuckle at the tail base, cannot be gripped by a tailer. I am not at all

19 Above - *the tail of grilse. No knuckle to tail*
Below - *tail of two sea-winter salmon. Note knobs of gristle above and below — the wire noose will tighten in front of these swellings.*

20 *(left) The tailer in use. If this had been a heavy salmon the tailer handle would have been pulled out of the author's hand as the strap is free.*

keen on the tailer as a piece of equipment. It is no easy matter to work one's hand through the leather strap whilst playing a fish; this strap is a safety measure ensuring that the handle is not pulled out of one's grip. In addition, it is hard to re-set the noose if it does not obtain a firm hold at the first attempt. A failed effort results in the angler holding the rod in one hand and in the other a 'sprung' tailer; without a third hand it is impossible to operate the reel on the rod and re-set the noose. To prevent these problems carry a tailer set up, with the noose over your head and left shoulder and passed under your right armpit. In this way you won't be strangled and it is almost ready for use. I once nearly lost a very good spring fish because I didn't put my hand through the leather wrist-strap, as the following fishing diary entry records:

21 March 1970. River Taw. Rising Sun water. Three R's Pool. River 2 ft 9 in., coloured. A warm soft day. 18 lb Salmon. 10.30 am. 2½ in. metal Yellow Belly Devon minnow. Lost grip and tailer went away with fish. Worked fish back and retrieved tailer: lifted fish by cable which slipped off and all fell in river. Tailed fish by hand. Retrieved tailer from bottom of river.

21 *Homemade gaff shaft. Champagne cork protects needle-sharp point. Gaff illegal on some rivers.*

I must admit that the fault was mine in the first place for not using the leather strap over my wrist, but it was one more thing to do when preoccupied with a heavy salmon in a full river. I still remember the fight very clearly. The salmon would not stop backing down the river. It would neither halt mid-stream, go up or across. Just down. And down and down we went until we almost reached the cable trolly, which will be well known by habitués of that water. I could go no further and it became a case of 'pull devil, pull baker', and there I used the tailer. Unknown to me my wife Pamela had watched the battle. Together we admired the curved, firm silver sea-liced body on the green spring grass.

The gaff

This is a barbless metal hook with a gape of about 2½ in. The hook may be screwed into a wooden shaft of a length to suit the angler or bound to an ash

sapling cut from the hedge, giving it a total length of about 4 ft. Telescopic metal gaffs are the best choice for a man fishing alone because they may be clipped to the trouser belt. Extended length is usually in the region of 40 in. and closed 20 in. Play out the salmon and with the rod in the left hand draw the fish across your front with its head to the left. If the rod is in your right hand the fish must approach from the angler's left, in which hand the gaff will be held. The 'rod in left hand' approach will be used if fishing from the right bank of a river; the 'rod in right hand' if fishing from the left bank. In both cases keep the nylon leader away from your gaffing arm.

The hook is placed over the back of the salmon at the front of the dorsal fin; the point, which must be needle-sharp, is then drawn into the salmon's flank; the fish may now be lifted from the river, swung ashore and hit on the head with the priest. It is a mistake to attempt to gaff a fish which is deep in the river; for distance, depth and aim are hard to judge. It is also a mistake to attempt to lift the head of the fish out of the water by rod pressure; no useful purpose is served by this action and the added strain may pull out the hook. It is possible to slip the point of the hook through the thin skin in the floor of the lower jaw of the salmon's mouth to save damage to the body of the fish. This action is only possible with a salmon which is entirely played out (I learnt to do this on pike, which have a large shovel of a mouth and give up the battle more readily than salmon).

Do not offer to gaff the fish of another angler unless he requests your help; in that event wait until the fish is played out before calmly attending to the mat-ter—let the fish pass by if it is too active, for there is nothing worse than losing another man's salmon.

In days gone by the gaff was king: gillies used them (and still do), and I always carried a telescopic one for the first 20 years of my fishing. I threw mine away when the cork handle broke as the result of my coshing salmon—in the closed position I used the gaff as a priest after the fish had been swung ashore. Today the gaff is not for me, and on some rivers it is illegal to carry one at any time. On others it may be prohibited before 1 April to save the kelts, and after the end of August to ensure a gravid hen may be returned undamaged. The only circumstance in which I would now carry a gaff would be in a big fish river. However, the chances of an angler meeting a salmon of 30 lb or more today in Britain are slim.

The net

The net is the best method of landing a fish if you cannot beach him and complete the capture with your hand. The fish is undamaged, and once inside the bag, which should be at least 2 ft 6 in. deep, he is yours. But there are two requirements: the net, when carried, must not be in the way as you fish or play a fish, and it must be large. By large I mean ample in the diameter of the ring or mouth which should be not less than 22 in. across. A small net will only accommodate a small fish, but a large one will accept both small and large victims.

Some people go out with a so-called grilse net with arms that lift, spread and clip open in the shape of a Y. In no circumstances take such a net salmon

22   *Gye net carried across the back in a leather peal sling. The shaft of this net has been shortened by 6 in.*

Purchase a Gye net, or as it may now be called a Rapier Gye, with a 24 in. ring of metal and a shaft that slides across the mouth when being carried on your back. The shaft is 48 in. long and this, together with the net ring, gives an extended length of 72 in. The net is carried across the back by a leather peal sling, which has a quick release tag. The only criticism I have of the shaft is that it protrudes above the anglers' shoulder when carried and this, coupled with the handle which sticks out slightly below the waist, makes it difficult to climb through bushes or trees when following salmon. I cut off the top 6 in. of the shaft and fit a split pin at the end as a stop—this done I find I can follow a salmon without impediment. The ring of the net when new is of bright aluminium; the glint of this may stimulate a fish to one further effort to escape. Spray the ring black or dark green with green car paint.

As to the actual netting, leave the Gye on your back until the fish is played out—be certain of this for it is extremely difficult to pursue a salmon downriver with the rod in one hand, net in the other and no third hand with which to operate the reel. So play him out. You should have already selected a quiet backwater into which to manouevre the tired salmon, for in a still area without current a salmon loses direction, flounders and is easily netted.

I like to enter the river, dropping down as close as possible to the level of the salmon. If you are fishing from the left bank take the rod in your right hand and the net in the left; with the butt of the rod inside your right thigh for leverage, work the salmon upstream, turn him, then swim him down headfirst into the net, which will be waiting below the surface. Once engulfed inside you

fishing: the arms may fail to open for various reasons or to lock into position when open, and the cord which crosses the front may sag under the weight of a fish, allowing it to slide out. Additionally the grilse net, by definition, is for a small one sea-winter salmon, causing you problems if you land two and three sea-winter fish.

23 *A salmon is in this net. Do not lift by the shaft or it will bend — draw it to the bank.*

24 *The net may then be held by the ring and the fish lifted onto the bank.*

may regain the bank at leisure drawing the fish after you, for the shaft of aluminium is soft, will easily bend and is not intended for lifting the salmon out of the water at arm's length. If fishing from the right bank the rod would be taken in the left hand. Either way the point is to ensure that the salmon swims down head first into the net because the current will then wash him in and the nylon leader will lie back along his body.

It is dangerous to attempt to net a salmon by drawing him upstream to the rim of the net. The first item to be encountered will be the fly leader or spinning trace, and a free hook of a

25b *If Bill Waldron lifted the net the shaft would bend.*

25a *The same angler in 1924 — R. Gairn — tributary of the Aberdeenshire Dee.*

26   *This salmon has been correctly netted — head first.*

treble, if outside the fish's mouth, may catch in the net mesh, jerking the other hooks free. At times one is forced to net a fish tail first, a risky task, for a slash of the tail will propel him straight out; if you must take him this way be sure his chin is just below the inside of the net ring and all of him in the bag before you lift.

I rarely hold the shaft by the hand grip at the end, but usually take hold about one foot from the ring or even grip the ring bracket itself. A floating net bag is a nuisance; it can be submerged by your dropping a stone into the bottom or better still, attach a strip of lead or copper to the bottom of the bag.

If an assistant is netting for you, be certain that you can see what is going on and drop the point of the rod as the fish enters the net—continued pressure might draw the salmon out. With a little practice it is easier to net a salmon alone as co-ordination between two people may not be exact.

The priest

To administer the last rites it is as well to carry a priest with you at all times. I use 8 in. of $\frac{1}{2}$ in. iron steam pipe. This simple cosh has a split ring in one end to which is attached a cord to encircle my neck and reach down to the priest, which I slip into my right-hand trouser pocket.

At times you may net a salmon in an awkward place, or beach the fish on a mid-stream, half-submerged rock; you have only a few seconds to withdraw the priest, administer a couple of thumps to the top of the salmon's skull and then sort out your position.

3 Fly-fishing equipment

The double-handed rod

One very wet afternoon in 1974 I parked my car close to the river, which was running high after a heavy rainfall. The flow, clearing by the hour, was turning to that deep whisky colour, from the hidden depths of which a salmon will appear at one's fly with a startling surge. When this happens there is an eye-widening moment of surprise, suspense and satisfaction whilst he is visible, followed by doubt that he has taken, then the rod-bending certainty that he has!

I set up a 12 ft split-cane rod — this was a time before I switched to carbon fibre — drew 9 ft of 17 lb Platil Strong nylon from a spool in my pocket to make a leader, and tied on a No. 1/0 single-hooked Hairy Mary (a hook I would not use today). After 100 yd of casting I had the faintest suspicion that a patch of water had lightened moment-arily, 3 or 4 ft below the fly, but as several more casts brought no response I continued on down the pool. Near the tail a salmon pierced the rolling waves as it took the natural bucktail fly; he came to the net after a sharp struggle in the rain and wind, during which I was constantly on the alert to persuade him not to run out of the tail of the pool. I carried the rather dark fish of 10 lb back to the car before returning once more to cast again over the lie

where the patch of water had lightened for a second or two. I was right, it had been a fish, and this time he would have the fly with no competitor to beat him to it as he took in a fast broad curve and went down; and down he stayed having taken a turn around a rock. I was well and truly snagged, and for the moment he had the better of me. He was large for that river, the rock was solid, the taut unfeeling line gave no hope or clue, and I was stuck upon the bank feeling miserable and fed up. But I had him, all 15 lb from the hooked kype to the lashing tail, when I plucked up courage, waded out into the dark water and lifted the line over the rock with the long rod. The nylon had held, the hook had not bent, and the salmon had not worked itself into a frenzy.

Half a mile below this a 6 lb grilse became attached and ran out of the tail of a fast pool. I was able to follow, lifting the line over the bushes growing on the bank.

These incidents illustrate three essential tools in river salmon fishing: a first-class hook which does not bend open, strong nylon of the best quality and a long rod in relation to the width of the river. The large salmon would have been lost on a 9 ft rod with which it would not have been possible to clear the line from the rock, and the same applies to the grilse if I had been unable to clear the bushes. Of course 12 ft was only long in relation to that small river. On wider waters 14 or 15 ft would be more appropriate.

What is the ideal design of a double-handed salmon rod? It must be:

1 Sufficiently stiff to cast accurately, against the wind, and to control a salmon;
2 from 12–15 ft in length;
3 light in weight and well-balanced.

These attributes will enable the fly to be moved over the water surface by mending the line (see p. 85, Fig. 77); the angler will not tire of casting but enjoy it; a fish may be controlled with the rod held high, leaving little line in the water to snag an obstruction; and the line may be cleared from river rocks and lifted over bankside bushes.

27 *Butt of 12 ft double-handed salmon fly-rod.*

Rods today are made of three materials: split cane (preferably resin-impregnated), fibreglass and carbon fibre. The rods will weigh as follows:

Split cane	12 ft 00 in. spliced	15 oz.
	12 ft 00 in. ferruled	16 oz.
	13 ft 00 in. spliced	17½ oz.
Fibreglass	12 ft 6 in.	14 oz.
	14 ft 00 in.	19 oz.
Carbon fibre	12 ft 6 in.	10 oz.
	14 ft 00 in.	13 oz.
	15 ft 4 in.	14 oz.

There is no doubt that carbon fibre is the most efficient, being the lightest for a given length, and owing to the narrow diameter of the tube less power is needed to cast against the wind than with fibreglass and split cane. However, we have to consider our pocket: fibreglass will be about half the cost of carbon fibre, which costs the same as split cane.

I like a rod to have a soul or personality, not to be one of thousands of

uniform tubes; to be of a natural material used in a country place. Thus by the smaller rivers, in defiance of my rational self, I will at times be found with a 12 ft spliced Sharpe's split cane, on which it is a delight to play a salmon, for the lack of ferruled or spigot joints allows an even bending in action. The dark colour of this cane, and the matt unvarnished finish, suit my constant desire to be unnoticed by the salmon I am stalking on the smaller streams. Yet carrying a 15 ft split cane is a man killer — half a day on the Welsh Dee with such a rod brought me to a full stop.

The single-handed rod

Because of the advantages of the long, double-handed rod I can find little to commend in the shorter single-handed salmon rod. You will lose fish upon them. You will also have to false cast to put out a long throw; this scares fish as the line flashes backwards and forwards over the lie. A double-handed rod will lay out the next throw without a false cast.

Despite these drawbacks many anglers use single-handed rods on small rivers in low water summer conditions, and they are essential in a boat. Even so, it is still sensible to use as long a rod as you can manage with comfort — at least 10 ft in carbon fibre. A 10 ft 6 in. or 11 ft rod in graphite weighs only 4 oz. to $4\frac{1}{2}$ oz. and may be fitted with a 4 in. push-in or screw-in extension handle. This extension, tucked into the stomach

28   *Single-handed 10 ft 6 in. fly-rod with butt extension fitted.*

29 *Single-handed fly-rod. Butt exten-sion removed.*

30 *Sharpe's 10 ft Seatrout Special split-cane fly-rod with 2 in. built-on extension.*

will take the weight off your wrist when playing a salmon. As the length of the extension is of no assistance in casting and, if excessive, line may catch under it when shooting extra length, it is best kept to the minimum necessary to support the wrist. The impregnated cane 10 ft Seatrout Special (designed by Hugh Falkus) has a built on 2 in. extension, and the 9 oz. weight of the rod is not excessive. Regretfully, such a rod, although capable of handling all sea trout and salmon under low water conditions with a floating line, is too heavy for most women. It was designed by a fisherman, looks right, is right, and once again is one of the few modern rods of soul and character.

The fly-reel

Use a large simple reel. One of aluminium alloy of $3\frac{7}{8}$ in. diameter will suit a 12 ft or 13 ft rod taking a No. 8 or No. 9 double taper line and 100 yd monofilament backing. For a rod above that length with a No. 10 or No. 11 line, a reel of 4 in. with a wide drum is required. Reels should have an adjustable drag and carry a spare ratchet spring in the back—a matter of some moment if such a spring were to break when on holiday in the Hebrides! Good reels are an investment. I have on my desk as I write a Hardy's invoice dated 6 February 1958. Among the items is a St John reel charged at £5. 0. 0d. I have that reel in use today and with it landed all my salmon from the time of purchase to 1980; it now belongs to my daughter to match her 12 ft carbon rod. In 1986 the same new reel was priced at £48.20. Incidentally I was invoiced £22. 12. 6d for a 2 top 12 ft A H E Wood No. 2

split-cane rod. A new rod of this sort would probably cost over £300 today. So it is better to make a good investment that lasts a life-time than buy second best tools that may feel inferior, bring less pleasure, and possibly let you down at a crucial moment.

The purpose of a large diameter is not only to take the required length of fly-line and backing but to recover that line as rapidly as possible when playing a fish — to this end it is essential to fill the spool almost, but not quite, to capacity. If a spool is only half-filled you might as well have a smaller reel. The models I suggested have the capacity to accommodate a 27 yd double taper floating line and 100 yd of 20 lb monofilament backing, or rather less if braided Dacron is used. A sinking line of the same AFTM (Association of Fishing Tackle Manufacturers) number will take up less room and therefore more backing will be required underneath the line to ensure a full spool. If you have purchased backing in 100 yd spools, and find the bulk insufficient, add a layer of old fly-line with a braided Dacron core next to the spool base. The most accurate way to fill the spool is to wind on the new line first, then the backing and any necessary old line until the spool is full — then draw off and reverse the whole. Most fly-reels have removable spools which may be released by a small catch at the centre — a pair of spools will take both floating and sinking lines without the necessity of purchasing more than one reel housing.

Beware of multiplying salmon fly-reels — the more moving parts, the more there is to go wrong. You may have discovered this if you have put your rod down on a sandbank in heavy rain and found the sand grains have

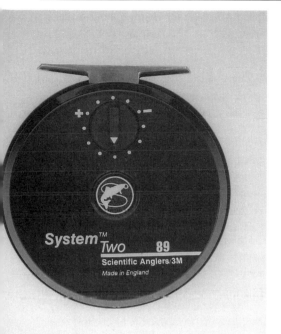

31   *The Scientific Anglers fly-reel System Two has an adjustable disc brake drag, exposed rim for additional finger braking, and quick release spools.*

splashed onto the reel, causing a jam. A multiplying reel with a few hidden grains of sand in the gears may lose you a salmon of greater value than the reel!

Without doubt the old Hardy Perfect $3\frac{3}{4}$ in. with a wide drum was ideal for salmon — buy one second-hand if it comes your way because they never wear out. Sadly, Perfects are no longer made above $3\frac{5}{8}$ in. diameter with a narrow drum, and this is just too small for our modern floating salmon lines.

Fly-lines

It is clear that a powerful rod will require a heavy line to bring out its capabilities, whilst a delicate wand would be overburdened by the same line and thus need something lighter. The fly-line manufacturers cater for these requirements, making lines of different weights coded internationally by the AFTM Scale; this is based upon the weight of the first 30 ft of the line excluding the thin 2 ft tip. It is not necessary for the angler to know the weights of lines in grains but he ought to appreciate that for practical purposes in salmon fishing he is likely to be using lines heavier than for smaller trout rods and that they will be coded in the range No. 7 to No. 11 — the larger number being the heavier. Thus a single-handed rod of 10 ft may require a No. 7 or No. 8 line, a double-handed rod of 12 ft 6 in. a No. 8 or No. 9, and a 14 ft weapon a line rated at No. 10 or No. 11.

Modern fly-rods are usually marked just above the handle with the line number considered most suitable by the manufacturers. This suggestion is based upon the weight of the first 30 ft of the line as we have already seen. This length was chosen as the average length of line false-cast by the average angler, but it may vary according to the circumstances of the fishing and only applies to the length of line held outside the rod tip. If you are normally casting a short distance, it would be reasonable to increase the line weight by one number on the scale — thus when sea trout fishing at night, when casting a short distance, a No. 8 line may balance a No. 7 rod. Much of my salmon fishing is done with a light 12 ft carbon rod rated at No. 9; on this I use a No. 8 line as I may extend a greater length when casting in situations where a 14 ft rod would be justified. I prefer the shorter rod for its greater delicacy.

Fly-lines are generally 27 yd in length, but AFTM ratings of 10 and above are available in 40 yd. The lines are tapered towards the tip where they are attached to the leader. This tapering avoids a marked 'step down' in diameter from the line to the thinner nylon leader, and makes possible accurate and delicate casting. Various line profiles are available: double taper, weight forward and shooting head. So far as salmon fishing is concerned no one other than a very skilled operator in exceptional circumstances, need consider any line other than a double taper. This line is suitable for overhead, roll and Spey casts, and when one end is worn out the line may be reversed upon the reel and the other taper end brought into use — two lines for the price of one!

Two lines are essential: a floater and a fast sinker. To this some anglers would add a floating line with a sinking tip to ensure that the fly does not skate on the surface of the water. The floating line floats because it is ligher than water; it does not need greasing to make it

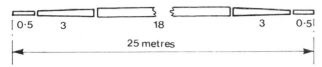

|0·5   3   18   3   0·5|

25 metres

32 *Profile of a double-tapered fly-line. There is little need in salmon and sea-trout fishing for the angler to concern himself with weight forward lines and shooting heads.*

float — greasing is a habit left over from the days when lines were made of dressed silk. Such a practice today is not necessary and if carried out will damage the plastic coating of the line, which may then crack, rapidly deteriorate and sink.

A sinker is heavier than water, and the heavier it is per unit of volume (more dense) the faster the rate at which it will go down. In a river, where the current is lifting the line downstream of the angler up to the surface, a slow sinking line will fish one foot down and a fast sinker two feet or more below the surface.

The lines available from a tackle dealer can be categorized as follows:

DT8F - a double-tapered AFTM No. 8 floating line

DT8S - a double-tapered AFTM No. 8 sinking line

DT8F/S - a double-tapered AFTM No. 8 sink tip line

In the case of the sinking lines the speed at which they sink is usually noted on the packet, i.e. fast, intermediate or slow. Neutral density lines fish in the surface film.

Line colour
A dark line, brown or deep green, seems less obtrusive under water and should be chosen for a sinker. So far as floaters are concerned, I went through a stage 20 years ago of using white lines, following the supposition that sea gulls had white bellies and were thus less likely to be seen from below — it was the fashionable theory at that time, rather inadequately based, for many birds have bellies of dark feathers. I caught salmon on these white lines, but probably less than I would have gathered using a dark shade. White lines flash in the sky over salmon lies — you can see them clearly when watching an angler from a distance, and white shows up more than brown or green on the water surface mirror when seen from below. I discarded white over 10 years ago in favour of green. I once purchased a very expensive mahogany-coloured floater on the basis that it fitted in with an unobtrusive matt rod, a sunburned face and drab clothing. It was almost invisible on the dark water and I had to discard it because I couldn't even see the position of my fly.

Knots
Backing to the fly-line has already been mentioned. On a salmon reel use 100 yd of 20 lb monofilament needle knotted to the line. A needle knot will slide out through the rod rings without jamming in the tip ring. If you use braided backing join it to the fly-line with the Albright knot — this is more bulky, however,

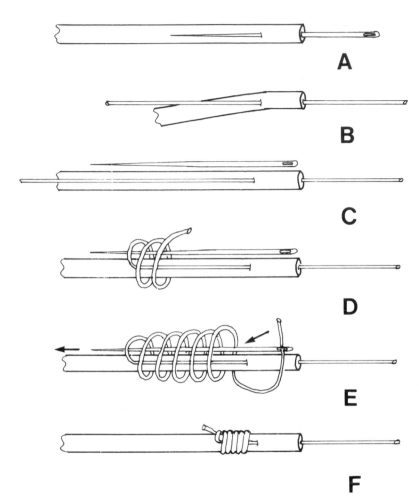

A

B

C

D

E

F

33   *The needle knot. Used to join mon-ofilament backing to the rear end of the fly-line. Also used to attach a short length, about one foot, of 20 lb monofilament to the front end of a fly-line to which the leader would be joined by a blood knot.*
A.   *Push a darning needle up the fly line centre for 5 mm and out through the side. Withdraw needle.*
B.   *Cut the forward end of the backing monofilament on a slant; this will help you thread the monofilament about 10 mm into the end of the line and then out of the side.*

C.   *Place the needle alongside the fly-line with the eye next to the end.*
D.   *Take five turns of the monofilament around the fly-line and needle, holding the coils side by side under a thumb.*
E.   *Keeping the backing under the thumb, thread the end through the needle eye and draw under the five turns that are still invisible under the thumb.*
F.   *Still holding the thumb over the coils, pull at each end of the backing. Remove thumb and adjust coils into even position before final tightening. Cut off waste end, which may protrude by about 2 mm.*

34 *Albright knot. To join braided backing to a fly-line. This knot is more bulky than a needle knot.*

than monofilament and the needle knot. Monofilament takes up less room, allowing a greater length on the reel; also, because of its smaller diameter and water-proof nature, there is less drag under the water surface when playing a fish if the backing has been run out.

The leader

Simple tackle is one of the joys of a day on a salmon river when fishing the fly. Rod, reel, net, half a dozen flies in a wallet and a spool of nylon are all you require. Pockets only are needed — do not take a bag.

The nylon must be of the best and, as with most things, you get what you pay for. I use 15 lb Platil Strong, which is 0·30 mm in diameter, on almost all occasions. I might reduce to 13 lb, 0·28 mm for the smaller flies — say a No. 6 or No. 8 low water hook. This nylon is expensive, but what is an extra £1 or £2 per 100 yd when related to the satisfaction of taking a salmon? I see from my fishing catalogues that many nylons of the same strengths have diameters greater by 0·07 mm. I can say with absolute honesty that I have not lost a salmon through nylon breakage on the fly in the 15 years that I have exclusively used Platil Strong. Of course I have lost fish which have come unstuck — but not through nylon breakage. I once had

to cut the leader when a salmon went through a hole between two rocks, came out on the other side and remained there, tethered like a dog chained outside a kennel.

Until 1985 my leaders were of 17.6 lb, and sometimes 12.8 lb, but these classifications were then discontinued. I have now gone down to a new 15 lb, finding it entirely satisfactory in landing seven salmon at the end of last season. You can also buy 20 lb leaders; I gave such a spool to a friend who promptly took a fish of 10½ lb in clear water on a 1¼ in. Black Dart tube fly. So much for the supposed, and to my mind unsporting, necessity of fishing fine! As to the length of leader: draw off about 9 ft, make a blood bight loop and join to the fly-line with a sheet bend. Such a length on a 12 ft rod will enable a fish to be netted without risk of winding the Sheet Bend up to the rod tip. If a shorter rod is used it would be wise to needle knot a 1 ft length of 20 lb Platil Strong into the end of the fly line and join this with a Blood Knot to the 9 ft leader—the junctions may then be wound in, or drawn out by the fish, which must be worked up close to the shorter rod to be netted.

The salmon fly

There are two essentials. The first is for the salmon to take the fly: to this end we must consider colour, weight, diameter and length. The second is that the fish be hooked and remain attached until landed: for this achievement the type of hook will greatly increase or reduce the success rate above or below 50 per cent, which is about the level of a single hook. Add together these two requirements, incorporate them in one well-thought-out fly tied in a variety of sizes, and you

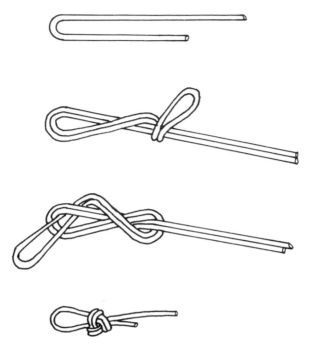

35   *Blood Bight Loop. To tie a loop on the end of a salmon leader.*

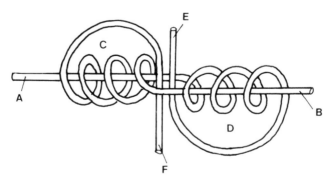

36   *Blood knot. To join lengths of nylon of the same diameter or lengths which are not too dissimilar. Start by overlapping ends e and f; twist e three times around b and f three times around a. Pull a and b to tighten loops c and d. Clip off e and* f to 2 mm. If a dropper is required leave 4 or 5 in. of e or f, being the end from the section closest to the fly-line — in this way, if a fish is taken on the dropper and the blood knot comes undone, the fish will still be attached.*

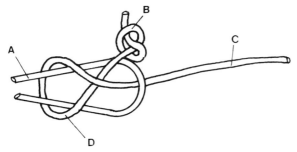

37 *Sheet Bend. To join the fly-line to a salmon leader when a long rod is in use. Tie knot b in fly-line, which is threaded through leader loop a as shown and loop d is tightened on leader by pulling c. To release push c towards a. For additional security an extra turn may be taken with d around a.*

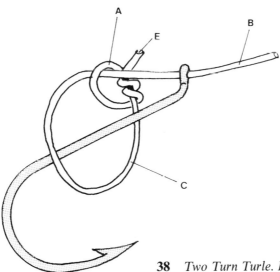

38 *Two Turn Turle. Eyed fly to leader. Tighten knot a on leader b and then pull b to tighten slip knot c on hook shank immediately behind eye of fly and in front of dressing. It makes a neat, streamlined job if end e is tucked under loop c before tightening — the end will then lie alongside the shank of the fly.*

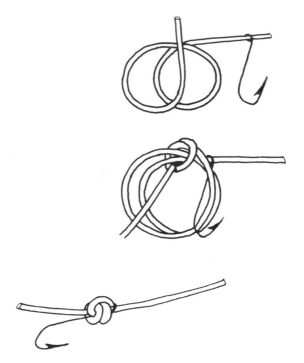

39   *Two Circle Turle. Large eyed fly to leader. Tie as two turn turle but with an extra coil as illustrated.*

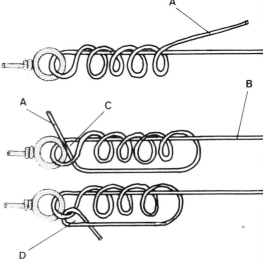

40   *Tucked Half Blood. Leader to tube fly treble, and nylon to swivels, baits, leads, etc. Thread nylon a through swivel ring or eye of treble hook, wind four turns around b, pass through aperture c in front of eye and then back through d. Tighten and cut off end to 4 mm. Tightening is assisted if the coils are moistened in the mouth.*

will land more salmon than would be yours on purchased flies. A further two advantages will accrue if these steps are taken: you will have faith in the fly which will remain in the water; good fishing time will not be wasted by constant changes. A salmon caught on a fly that you have designed and dressed yourself will bring great satisfaction — far more than a fish taken on a purchased lure.

Salmon can be caught on almost any salmon fly when they are in the mood, just as we have days and nights when trout and sea trout are almost suicidal — but when these excited moods are upon them the well-thought-out fly will hook and land even more, and when salmon are dour the only fish of the day may fall to the design which excites their curiosity. Here lie the secrets of the take: curiosity stimulated by colour and action; the surprising sudden appearance of an unusual object for a river situation; a little territorial aggression; and perhaps a momentarily awakened memory of past feeding in their early river life and in the sea. Add to these the excitement of a spate and anyone may prompt a salmon to grab the fly.

Of course the final secrets, the real truth of the matter will never be entirely known. What goes on in the salmon's head will remain a mystery to us. Much as we admire their complex life cycle and marine navigational ability, it may be that very little activity takes place in a salmon's head. In fact this must be so or a salmon would be driven frantic with frustration when forced by drought to remain in a particular lie for months on end waiting for a spate to enable them to continue their journey up the river, with only a few jumps and a cruise around the pool at dusk and dawn to relieve the grey monotony of life. It is rational to believe that the majority of the hours of night and day of their adult river life are spent in a state of torpor. The relieving of torpor by the arrival of extra water and the sudden startling appearance of a lure account for most takes, as we shall see — but correct fly design and colour help this stimulation.

Colour

It is established fact that salmon see in colour, as do trout and sea trout. When this became known Richard Walker designed a most successful trout lure — the Sweeney Todd. This fly is a combination of red and black with a black striped body; it has caught many trout in lakes and reservoirs. There is no doubt that it would catch salmon, but we would not fish it in the single hook form for we can do better. Richard Walker knew that fish see red, orange and yellow better than other colours, and stripes very clearly. As awareness of the lure must be half the battle, I set about the design of a fly to be called The Black Dart. No claim is made that miracles will be accomplished by this lure but it has proved effective in a number of rivers when other flies have failed to produce a response.

For this I decided to use a red or orange winged fly with stripes and the most contrasting of stripes, black and white. As well as catering for visual awareness it is necessary to excite the memory of feeding; at the same time fear must not be induced. I decided black and white in equal stripes would prove too startling, like a zebra crossing, and so I chose a black body with a gold or silver tinsel that glitters like little fish upon which salmon feed in the sea. Tinsel also protects the body silk, enabling the same fly to be used for two or three salmon. If the 'wing' of the fly is made of bucktail it will open and close when tweaked through the water, closely resembling a backing shrimp, prawn or squid. (Wing is misleading. There is no single wing in a tube fly — bucktail is tired on sparsely around the whole body, or in a tuft on two sides.) Finally, add a jungle cock eye at each side of the head. This feather is itself in the contrasting colours yellow, black and white.

Consider the success of the Peter Ross fly. This is a traditional trout, sea trout and salmon fly in which the wing has the light and dark stripes of the teal feather, the body is red with the stripes of silver tinsel ribbing and the tail is of golden-pheasant tippet fibres, which have the contrasting colours of orange with a black tip. That fly has stood the test of time, as has the Black Pennel — a black body with silver ribbing, very like the modern Black Chenille, and the Black Lure, which is a favourite sea trout fly. These highly successful traditionals, accidentally conforming to those colours recently established experimentally as desirable, confirm the shade requirements of the best salmon fly.

To crystallize the matter we need:
a black body striped with gold or silver tinsel;
a red or orange hair wing;
a jungle cock cheek.

Doubtless a man would do well, or better than most, who fished the season through with only two colours: *orange* for salmon and *black* for sea trout.

The hook
There is a wide choice of hooks on which to tie the coloured materials available. They come in several types:
the single hook;
the double hook;
the Waddington mount with treble hook;
the Esmond Drury and Partridge up-eyed treble hooks;
the tube with a treble hook.

From one or two of these we have to make up heavy enough flies to swim well without skating on the surface when fished with a floating fly-line; yet the lure must not be lifelessly heavy. A balance must therefore be achieved between weight and the water-flow resistance of the frontal area. A fat lightweight fly will ride up to the surface when held against the current. A fly with the correct weight/diameter ratio will fish just below, but not break, the water surface. The hook must also take a firm hold on a high percentage of those salmon taking it into their mouths, and they must stay attached until landed. Let us see how these hook and mount styles measure up to our requirements.

The single hook
Few people fish today for salmon with a single-hooked fly. Some of us cut our teeth on them as I did in my first full week at salmon on the fly in the 1950s when five fish came my way from the Helmsdale on a No. 6 Low Water single 'Hairy Mary' in June. The reasons are that the three-way hooking capacity of a treble takes a better hold in the fish's mouth, particularly when a gap forms behind the kype and between the jaws of a cock fish in autumn — a gap wide enough for a single to pass through at the moment of take, without catching. Additionally, many singles have a long shank which allows leverage on the hook hold. This leverage, from the changing directions of the line-pull during play, may work the hook loose in more cases than is acceptable. In one

season 20 years ago my favourite fly was a single hooked Thunder & Lightning in sizes No. 1/0, No. 2 No. 4 and No. 6 — all suitable for fishing in a spate. It was a drive of 110 miles to the river, making a round trip of 220 miles. During that season, on five consecutive visits, I lost after several minutes the only fish hooked — the fly just came unstuck. Without doubt the hook hold was such that the shank of the fly was outside the mouth of the fish — leverage from changing directions during the fight broke out the hold. I had driven 1100 miles for nothing other than experience gained. Slow to learn? Without doubt — but convinced. The lesson was rubbed in from time to time by breakages of fine metal, long shanked, low water hooks, which broke under the severe stress of a line fouled around a rock.

If you were spinning for mackerel with a spoon bait or for salmon with a Devon minnow you would discard the mount if one of the treble points were broken, let alone two points, so why fish voluntarily with a single? Well, there are two advantages, although neither is great enough to persuade me to use them for salmon: the fly has a good weight/frontal area ratio, presenting little resistance to the water flow, it is also less likely to tangle on the leader. This last attribute really only concerns sea trout fishing at night when the fly cannot be seen — I will deal with this later.

The double hook

The double has the advantage of a little more weight than the single, and the two hooks are more likely to take an initial hold than one hook. However, in the case of doubles with long shanks, one hook may lever out the other when the leader pulls from varied directions whilst the salmon is being played. A small short-shanked double is preferable to a single if a treble-hooked fly is not available.

The Waddington

An excellent hooking mount on which to dress the fly. It consists of a wire the length of the fly, with a loop twisted at both ends; to one end is tied the leader whilst the other is passed through the eye of a ringed hook, before being twisted around the wire forming the shank. Such a device may be made with a paper clip but has the disadvantage that the fly has to be discarded if the hook is damaged. A better arrangement is marketed by Partridge in their Waddington shanks. These double-wire shanks have a small clip at the end so that when the dressing is complete the hook may be clipped on and the clip

41 *Partridge Waddington shank for salmon. If the hook is damaged a new hook may be fitted provided the dressing materials are not taken over the gap in one wire of the shank. Rubber cycle valve tubing keeps the treble hook in line with the fly body.*

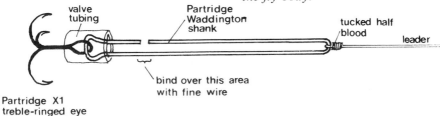

valve tubing   Partridge Waddington shank   tucked half blood   leader

bind over this area with fine wire

Partridge X1 treble-ringed eye

bound closed with fine wire. These shanks are available in lengths of ½ in. to 2½ in. There are two disadvantages: the treble will waggle or hang down at the end unless held in line with a piece of bicycle-valve rubber; and there is the possibility that the long-wire shank could exert leverage on the hook when twisted in certain directions when the fish is played.

The Esmond Drury and Partridge up-eyed trebles

These are very desirable treble hooks on which to dress your fly. They have slightly turned out points and an up eye. If dressed sparsely the weight/frontal area ratio is excellent and the fly will not skate, and swims well. The largest size, No. 2, may cause problems, for the shank lengthens, resulting in leverage, the weight increases substantially and the fly goes into the river with a plop. Mind your ears as a No. 2 whistles by!

The tube fly

There are convincing reasons for using tube flies for almost all salmon fishing. However, the polythene tube must have a socket at the tail into which to insert the eye of the treble hook, and the tube must be weighted or it will skate on the water surface. This weight may be

42   *Type B Slipstream socketed poly-thene tube for salmon and sea trout flies.*

provided by fine lead wire wrapped in side by side turns around the tube and beneath the dressing.

If you think the lead will make the tube too fat, a tapered brass collar may be slipped onto the nylon before the leader is passed through the tube; the collar will then rest in front as an addition to the head. A tube of brass would provide the necessary weight, and these are readily available, but socketed brass tubes do not seem to be on the market; in any case the hook eye would fall out, not being gripped as it is by the more elastic polythene tube.

If a tube is used without the socket the hook may stick out at right angles and catch on the leader. A 1 in. socketed tube is about the minimum length, or the fly, which must be on the stout side to provide the diameter for a socket, will be out of proportion in diameter to length. A 1¼ in. or 1½ in. fly is ideally shaped with regard to length and diameter.

The socketed tube is best used when there is plenty of water requiring a fly of one inch or above. In low clear warm water (summer fishing) this may be too large and in consequence forsaken for a small Esmond Drury rather than an unweighted slim short tube without a socket, or a low water single.

You now have to decide on a treble hook to suit the tube. When first dressing the 1 in. and 1¼ in. socketed tubes,

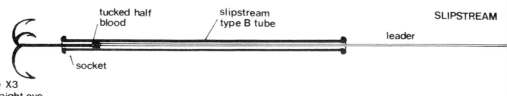

tucked half blood   slipstream type B tube   SLIPSTREAM

socket   leader

Partridge X3
treble-straight eye

which are called type B Slipstream and
marketed by E. Veniard Ltd, a No. 10
ringed treble was tried in which the
hook points were parallel with the central shank. None of the first half dozen
salmon hooked was lost but it was
noticeable that the hook had taken a
very shallow hold, owing to the small
gap by which it protruded outside the
fat tube. Next tried were No. 8's of the
same shape — the salmon took no
exception to this large size, even on a 1
in. fly, and most were landed.

A further improvement came with
No. 8 Partridge code X 3, short-shank,
outbend trebles. This is an ideal hook,
for the needle eye slides into the tube
socket, the outpoints have a slightly
greater hooking capacity than a treble
with parallel points, and the short shank
does not exert leverage against the hook
hold. The wire of this hook may appear
fine but, being of exceptional quality,
fish have not been lost by bending and
consequent widening of the gape. In
view of the small cost of a treble hook
in relation to the value to the angler of
a salmon, it is wise to fit a new hook to
the tube after each fish — an action not
readily accomplished with a Waddington unless of the hook clip variety, and
even then the clip has to be bound shut.

This highlights another advantage of
the tube fly — simple and rapid hook
replacement. The No. 8 code X3 suits
the 1, 1¼ and 1½ in. tubes, but a No. 6 is
suggested for the 2 in., which is the
longest made and would only be needed
for early spring or later autumn fishing,
or in high and dirty water conditions.

If the colour requirements outlined
earlier, the socketed type B Slipstream
tube and the Partridge code X3 hook,
are employed together, you have a fly
called the Black Dart. This fly has
accounted for many salmon on rivers

of varying character when fished by
anglers working their fly in a variety of
ways. Below is the dressing:

The Black Dart

Tube:	Type B Slipstream socketed
Hook:	1–1½ in. tubes No. 8, Partridge X3
	2 in. tube No. 6, Partridge X3
Tag:	No. 16 oval gold tinsel
Body:	Black floss over close turns of fine lead wire. The lead is stopped short of the head where the bucktail is to be tied in
Rib:	No. 16 oval gold tinsel
Wing:	Orange bucktail
Cheeks:	Jungle cock. A long feather, three-quarters the length of the tube - one on each side
Head:	Black varnish
Silk:	Black Naples

The one inch length has the least weight
but no less water resistance than the
longer tubes — consequently the one
inch fly will fish closest to the surface,
sometimes in the film itself. At times it
may be desirable, whilst using a floating
line, to swim a one inch tube 5 or 6 in.
down. For this situation a second fly
was evolved and called the Copper Dart.
It is slightly slimmer and heavier than
the Black Dart and is easy to dress.

The Copper Dart

Tube:	1 in. type B Slipstream socketed
Hook:	No. 8 Partridge X3, outpoint treble
Body:	Side-by-side turns of 0.40 mm copper wire over a single side-by-side layer of black Naples silk

Wing:	Orange bucktail
Cheeks:	Jungle cock. A feather three-quarters the length of the tube — one on each side
Head:	Black varnish
Silk:	Black Naples

The black Naples silk is run from the head down the length of the body to just above the socket opening where the copper wire is doubled under and tied in. The silk is then taken back to the head. The copper wire is then bound in side by side turns up to just behind the head, but stopped short of the point where the bucktail is to be tied down. It is as well not to dress a stock of the Copper Dart - just make one or two as required, for the copper oxidizes to a dull colour after some time and then no longer gives off an attractive glint in the water.

Small flies

There will be occasions in summer, in warm, low and clear water, when a small fly is needed. The socketed tube is unsuitable for this situation where the angler would do well to consider a No. 10 Partridge or Esmond Drury treble. A simple black striped body may be tied on with a wing of orange hair and jungle cock cheeks.

The Black and Orange fly

Hook:	No. 10 Esmond Drury treble or Partridge X2B
Body:	Black floss ribbed No. 16 oval silver tinsel
Wing:	Orange bucktail
Cheeks:	A small junge cock feather on each side
Head:	Black varnish
Silk:	Black Naples

There is also much to be said for a Stoat's Tail which may be dressed by adding two tufts of black hair, one on each side, just behind the eye of the hook. There is no need for a dressed body, but black floss may be added if desired.

The Stoat's Tail

Hook:	No. 12 Esmond Drury treble or Partridge X2B
Body:	Black floss silk
Wing:	Stoat or black labrador hair
Head:	Black varnish
Silk:	Black Naples

The shrimp fly as a 'dropper'

Hook:	No. 8, No. 10 or No. 12 Esmond Drury treble or Partridge X2B
Body:	Tail half in red floss, front half in black floss
Rib:	No. 16 oval silver tinsel
Throat hackle:	Hot orange
Cheeks:	Two small jungle cock feathers
Wing:	Orange bucktail
Head:	Red varnish

This fly is no exception to the rule that the colours red, orange and yellow should predominate. It may be fished very effectively in a small size as a dropper, to be scuttled across the surface of rough water at the neck of a pool. Salmon often come in such a place at the final moment of the cast as the angler is about to lift off; there may be some stimulation in the fly breaking from below, through the surface film, and then forming a vee of ripples on top of the water.

It is unwise to fish a dropper in a river with many snags and boulders, or with much weed, for if the trailing fly catches in a weed bed as the salmon fights into cover it may pull the dropper out of the salmon's mouth, or vice versa if the point fly has been taken. A dropper may also be fished with advantage from a boat using a long single-handed rod of 10–11 ft. — again the dropper is scuttled over the surface before lifting off into the back cast.

Alternative flies

There are occasions in both high and low water when a salmon is risen but will not come again to the same fly. Tempting such a fish by altering the movement of the fly will be discussed later, but a change of fly colour will sometimes, but not often, result in a firm take. It is worth a try. In low water there are the alternatives of Black and Orange fly and the Stoat's Tail. In high water, sufficient to warrant a $1\frac{1}{4}$ in. Black Dart, a Hairy Mary socketed tube of the same size should be given a swim over the lie of an interested salmon. The natural brown bucktail of this lure is less obtrusive than the orange of the Black Dart, just as is the case with the sombre Stoat's Tail in comparison with the Black and Orange fly. We know that the orange colour is the most visible, and is thus first choice; it has shown us the fish, but some salmon seem to prefer quieter colours which blend with the river.

The Hairy Mary

Tube:	$1\frac{1}{4}$ in. type B Slipstream socketed
Hook:	No. 8 Partridge X 3 treble outpoint
Tag:	No. 16 oval silver tinsel closest

to the socket and two or three turns of yellow floss above.

Body:	Black floss over side by side turns of fine lead wire
Rib:	No. 16 oval silver tinsel
Wing:	Natural brown bucktail
Head:	Black varnish
Silk:	Black Naples

The prawn fly

Tube:	$1\frac{1}{2}$ in. type B Slipstream socketed
Hook:	No. 8 Partridge X 3 outpoint treble
Body:	Single layer of hot orange silk covered with side by side turns of 0.40 mm copper wire. The wire is stopped $\frac{2}{3}$ in. short of the socket end to allow space for the head to be formed
Whisker:	Orange bucktail. A tuft is tied in pointing up the body towards the tail, and then doubled over and tied down just behind the socket mouth. This doubling forms the prawn's head carapace. The turned-over bucktail fibres continue as the whiskers.
Eyes:	Two very small jungle cock feathers
Silk:	Hot orange

There are narrow gorges in some rivers where salmon lie below the main rush of water which passes over their heads, and through which they may not readily come up to take a fly fished on a floating line. It is common practice to obtain success in such places by spinning; the bait being kept down by a lead weight. For the man who wishes to fish solely with a fly-rod the copper-bodied prawn fly may tempt a salmon. It must be fished deep, and very slowly let down the pool on a fast-sinking line. No attempt has been made in the dressing of this fly to provide the body with legs or a tail — just jungle cock eyes and a single tuft of orange bucktail on top.

This bucktail head and whiskers act as a rudder at the downstream end, keeping the fly horizontal and in line with the current. The socket of the tube is, of course, at the head where the hook sits hidden in the whiskers. The nylon leader enters through the unadorned tail end.

4 Fly-fishing

Casting

Face downstream towards the sea: the right bank is on your right hand side and the left bank is to your left. This is the same in all rivers. The knowledge is necessary to understand the casting techniques for double-handed salmon fly-rods. Single-handed casts will not be covered in this book for they are basic to trout fishing, at which the angler should already be competent before

attempting salmon and sea trout fishing. If one cannot cast well by day for trout it is certainly too soon to consider sea trout fishing at night when one must handle the tackle in the dark.

The overhead cast

This is the most widely used of the double-handed casts, but it relies upon sufficient space behind and above the angler for the line to straighten in the air to his rear. The cast should be learned with the right hand up for

43 *Correct casting position.*

44   *Awkward casting position.*

fishing from the left bank, and the left hand up when fishing from the right bank.

In figure 43 the angler is facing downstream on the right bank left hand up. In figure 44 he has his right hand up— this is clearly awkward unless the angler faces across the river. Learn to cast with either hand up the rod. Figures 45–54 show the sequence for overhead casting. It will be noted in this sequence that no false cast has been included. The height of a salmon rod and the length of line it will handle make false casting largely unnecessary. At the end of a cast draw in 2–3 yd of line over the forefinger of the hand which is up the rod - this loop should be retained under the finger and shot on the forward cast. Never let go of this loop as the rod goes into the back cast or all the power needed to lift

the line will be dissipated in taking up the slack of this loop. False casting over the river frightens salmon — avoid it. False casting is only necessary to extend line when using a short single-handed rod; this also should be avoided when salmon fishing on rivers. I have no doubt that false casts scare fish. When after trout in a lake a fish will often boil at the water surface as it dives hurriedly to cover from a position below a line shooting out in the air.

In the overhead cast if a crack is heard in the air behind the caster this is due to starting the forward cast before the back cast has straightened. To cure this make a longer pause with the rod just past the vertical to give the line more time to straighten in the air behind the angler and more power to enable it to do so.

When fishing a river and you want to change the position of the fly from the

45 *End of previous cast.*

46 *Loop of line has been drawn in by left hand over right forefinger: rod is starting to lift line.*

47   *Further lift.*

48   *More lift and power to accelerate line into back cast.*

49 *Rod stopped just past the vertical; butt close to chest in left hand prevents rod going back too far.*

50 *Rod remains in same position, but line has straightened behind as angler pauses.*

51 *Power applied forward by right hand only, left hand stationary as pivot.*

52 *Line commences to straighten in front, angler aims at far bank above water level, shoots the slack by releasing right forefinger at final moment as line is straight and about to drop.*

53 *Right forefinger collects line again.*   **54** *Left hand takes in any slack over right forefinger to re-establish contact with fly.*

dangle at the end of the previous cast to a point almost opposite to the angler proceed as follows, bring the rod through 90° until it points to the required place whilst still parallel with the water, then go into the back cast. At all times keep the hand on the butt close to the chest — the butt hand acts as a pivot; it should not be moved more than 5 or 6 in. out from the body. If the caster finds his rod is travelling too far back past the vertical on the back cast, because his body is bending backwards, he must move forward the foot on the same side as that from which the cast is being made. This will produce a more aggressive forward leaning stance.

The roll cast

This cast should be learned before the Spey casts. Its uses are to throw out the line without lifting it into the air behind the angler: this is necessary if there is a tree or high bank to the rear which precludes the use of the overhead cast. It is also useful when fishing the sunk line, to raise the line from the water with a roll before lifting off into the back cast of the overhead sequence. The roll cast by itself does not enable the angler to make any great change in the direction of the new cast from the position at the termination of the previous cast — for this we need either the overhead or one of the Spey casts.

The sequence is illustrated in figures 55–59.

55 *The start.*

56 *The rod is raised until it is just past the vertical and a loop of line is hanging behind the angler as in fig. 62.*

57 *At this point the right hand snaps hard forward with a power that one might feel would break the rod.*

58   *The line rolls forward...*   **59**   *and straightens.*

The single Spey
This cast is used when the angler cannot raise the line into the air above or behind him, owing to obstructions such as cliffs or trees, and he wishes to change the position of his fly from 'on the dangle', at the end of the previous cast, to the other side of the river. The cast may be made when the wind blows upstream, or if there is no wind at all; but it cannot be executed in a strong downstream wind. When fishing from the right bank the left hand should be up the rod; if from the left bank the right hand should be up. In both cases the angler faces downstream with his legs at right angles to the bank. The sequence is illustrated in figures 60 66.

60 *Angler on right bank facing downstream, left hand up, feet at right angles to bank.*

61   *Rod is raised almost to vertical and then swung sharply out over the river, lifting the line and scuttling the fly upriver over the surface until ...*

62   *the fly and the line fall on the water just upstream of the angler.*

63 *Angler commences forward punch;*   **64** *power continues from left arm;*

65   *rod stops here; line comes over;*   **66**   *straightens in the air; and then falls on the river.*

The double Spey

Used for the same purpose as the single Spey, but when a strong downstream wind makes it impossible for the angler to drop the line on the water upstream of his position. When fishing from the right bank the right hand should be up the rod, and when on the left bank the left hand should be up. The feet are placed parallel to the bank and the angler faces straight across the river. The sequence is shown in figures 67–75.

There is no doubt that to learn these casts an angler would be well-advised to take instruction from a professional. Unless the actions are mastered the angler will find himself unable to fish all waters. Before I learned the Speys I remember fishing the left bank of a pool during the run-off of a spate that made my mouth water. The atmosphere, the whole river, everything, smelled of salmon. I could imagine my triumphant hand on the grey slippery side of a netted fish—and then one sloshed!

It was a large fish, thick, curved, broad tailed and all of 20 lb. Very desirable. He was in a high water lie at the tail of the pool under the far bank. That should present no problem, I thought: an overhead cast, a mend, a long slow rolling rise and 'Bob's your Uncle', but there was a line of trees behind me! I did everything but place my fly over that salmon which continued to show. It was all my own fault because I had thought Spey casting unnecessary, a fancy cast not required by a practical, down-to-earth fisherman. I never caught the fish, of course, but I made my way rapidly to a casting instructor.

67 *Angler on right bank, right hand up, faces far bank, feet parallel to own bank.*

68 *Raises rod almost to vertical; line* **69** *Swings rod out over river until...*
still straight downstream.

70 *it points upstream.*   **71** *Rod then swung downstream.*

72   *Line curves in front of, and then falls*   **73**   *who commences forward snap.*
in loop behind and to the right of angler ...

74 *Line curves out and...*

75 *straightens in the air before falling on the water.*

Sinking line

In cold water salmon stay deep in the river and it is uncommon for them to rise close to the surface to take a fly. Consequently, it is necessary to use a sinking fly-line that will take the fly down to the depth we require; this should be as close to the level occupied by the salmon as it is possible for us to achieve against the lifting effect of the river current. The fly must also be fished as slowly as possible, consistent with life-like movement. In the cold salmon are slow to move and slow to make up their minds!

76　*A 12-pounder taken in March by the author on a sunk fly-line. Net ring supported by two hands to lift ashore.*

Benefits will follow the carrying of a pocket thermometer when fishing in early spring in February, March and the first half of April. There are models designed for anglers in which the glass tube is protected by a brass case that has a small window through which to see the scale, and a loop at the end by which it may be suspended in the river on a cord. Below a water temperature of 45°F use a fast-sinking fly-line. Continue with this line up to a temperature of 48°F or 50°F if there is plenty of water in the river, for the flow will be at a fast speed and the fly must be held down. If the river is low when in the 45°F region a sink tip line may be used, or a slow sinker if you like to add this to your range of lines. Above 50°F adopt the floating line techniques to be discussed later: these will continue throughout the summer until the water once more cools in late autumn, when a sinking line will again be required.

These statements are perhaps too categorical on water temperature bands; there will always be exceptions as conditions of temperature, flow and water colour alter constantly. One of these exceptions is the use from time to time of the sinking line in summer when the water temperature is high. When to take off the floater and put on a sinker in summer is up to the angler at the time, for it is an unusual step to take, but there is much to be said for changing a losing game!

If you have to fish in July or August in bright weather, because you have paid your money and have no choice, and the floating line has not brought a reaction from the fish, then change to a sinking line with a larger fly than is suggested by the water temperature. You have nothing to lose by such an alteration and, by going down deep to torpid fish, may stir a take. At the very least the change will stimulate you to fish for a while with increased concentration. Don't forget that at one time there were no floating fly-lines, all lines sank unless greased, and greasing only commenced at the turn of this century. Plenty of fish were caught on these silk lines.

Not only must the density of the fly-line be considered and the amount by which you wish it to exceed the specific gravity of water (depth control), you must decide on the length of fly to be used and the weight of that fly. The word length is put forward rather than a hook size such as 1/0 or 2/0 in the large singles because most fishing in the early part of the year will be with heavy tube flies and Waddingtons; the large singles are inefficient in the hooking and landing of salmon, as already discussed. For a general starting point, the colder the water the longer the tube or, more accurately, the longer the whole fly from the head to the end of the hair or bucktail wing that hides the hook. At 40°F a socketed tube of 2 in. would be about right. This length of tube would give an overall fly measurement of $2\frac{1}{2}$ in. If the water is coloured heavily at this temperature a longer fly would be advisable — perhaps a $2\frac{1}{2}$ in. Waddington shank; such a fly would measure at least 3 in. when the hook is added. At 45°F in clear low water a $1\frac{1}{4}$ in. fly tube is probably acceptable to the fish, or $1\frac{1}{2}$ in. if the river is high and with a stain of colour. Both these measurements are of the tube excluding the hook.

The fly itself should not be excessively heavy to achieve depth. Instead gain depth by using the correct density line, casting and line movement techniques. Besides which, a very heavy fly is dang-

erous to cast overhead and does not move with life in the water. Few people take the trouble to inspect the way a fly swims in the current, but it may be observed, if a fly is hung in a deep clear current where it may be seen, that a heavy body hangs down at a sharp angle, whilst the bucktail streams out horizontally. To overcome this, add weight to the fly dressing closer to the head than the tail and use a lightweight hook.

The heavier the fly the stronger the nylon leader should be. As already mentioned 15 lb Platil Strong is suitable for most salmon flies, but in fishing the heavier lures of early spring it would be sensible to use a leader of 20 lb. This leader need not be long, 5 or 6 ft is quite sufficient because visibility and line shadow are not much of a problem at this time of year. It is usual to spin in spring with a 1 yd trace and a lump of lead to hold down the minnow — if salmon are not troubled by this they will certainly not be upset by a leader reduced from 9 to 5 ft in length. Heavy flies fished on fine nylon may 'crack off', and the whole will be unbalanced and more difficult to cast.

It is a great mistake and unsporting to use nylon of a fineness that may break. At times breakage may occur, owing to cutting on a rock or a mishap such as the occasional wind knot, but to intentionally fish finer nylon than could be used is foolish, and it is unjustifiable to see a salmon escape with a fly in the mouth owing to breakage. Wind knots should be spotted as soon as they occur because they reduce the nylon strength by 50 per cent. Cultivate a regular habit of glancing up the leader from the fly held in one hand to the end of the nylon near the rod tip that is pointed to the light of the sky — the small dot of a wind knot on the uniform smoothness of the leader will be clearly seen. Replace the leader from the spool of level nylon in your pocket; do not repair leaders for salmon.

If the angler has a choice of rods now is the time to use a long one of 14 or 15 ft - not because it is always necessary to cast a long distance (although the ability to do so is useful) for the fish may be under your own bank, but to assist in lifting the sunk fly-line from the water. It is asking a great deal of a 12 ft rod to lift a fast-sinking line out of the river all day long - the longer weapon will raise the line with ease to the river surface before comfortably executing a Spey cast, and the Spey cast it ought to be for safety to keep a large and heavy fly away from the fisherman. There is no joy in being hit on the head by a 3 in. tube travelling fast through the air on an overhead cast, for a very heavy fly is difficult to keep up on the back cast. If you must use an overhead cast with a heavy fly at least take the precaution of putting on a hat, turning up your collar and wearing polaroid spectacles.

The aim of most anglers at this time of year is to cast across the river at an angle of about 45° downstream and swim the fly to pass in front of a salmon as slowly as possible and as close in depth to the fish as we can achieve. In practice this means down almost to the bed of the river. The line having come across and straightened below you, and now being on the dangle, slowly hand in about 1 yd in small pulls before raising the rod to lift the line high in the water before the next cast. Salmon at times take during this 1 yd retrieve, but I have not found as many taken then as do so when the line is in a curve and just beginning to straighten below the angler.

To achieve depth and slow movement concentrate on casting and subsequent line control. It is obvious that a fly pivoting from a point out in the river will come across more slowly than if held from a point at the edge of the river or on the bank. It is therefore sensible to wade out if you are able to do so, and, having cast, to hold the rod over the water at right angles to the bank. On a small river wading out 2 yd and holding across a 15 ft rod towards the far bank, a total of 7 yd may be one quarter of the width of the water. But whatever the width, wading and rod holding at right angles will help the fly cross the river more slowly.

Additionally, an immediate upstream mend should be made when the cast alights on the water, before the river has time to take a hold on the line. If the angler moves downstream a step or two as soon as he has cast, this will give the line four or five seconds to sink before being held against the lifting water flow. (This is an alternative to the usual practice of moving down between casts.) A downstream step at the moment the fly-line alights on the river has the same effect as back winding when spinning to allow the minnow a second or two to sink before the retrieve commences. This initial mend is the only one the angler will be able to achieve, and the fly will now be moved across the river by the current. Soon after the fly has commenced its swim back across the river, the angler should start a slow movement of his rod to keep pace with the direction of the fly so that both fly and rod arrive in a line parallel with the bank at the same moment.

1

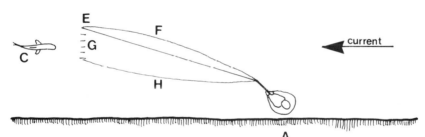

current →

2

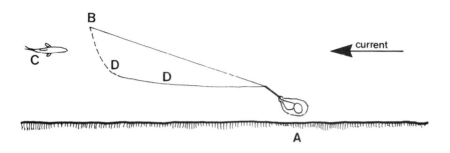

current →

77 *An upstream mend.* 1 *Angler casts from A to B hoping to rise the fish at C. The current presses on the fly line and sweeps the fly away too rapidly in curve D.* 2 *Angler casts to E and at once mends the line over to F without moving the final yard of the line, the leader and the fly, which remain at E. The fly will then swim slowly in path G across the front of the fish at C whilst the current is straightening the upstream curve F to almost straight line H. Mending is used to counteract the pull on the line of fast water — it is not necessary to mend in slow portions of the river where the requirement may be to speed up the fly.*

Experience and the requirements of different pools will establish the height at which the tip of the rod is held during the crossing of the river by the fly. Two factors are involved: the closer to the water the rod tip is held, the greater the downstream curve or belly will be in the line and the greater the speed (which is to be avoided) of the fly. The higher in the air the rod tip is held the less deep will the fly fish (and we need depth) but it will cross more slowly. These two factors seem irreconcilable, but a balance may be achieved. In fact, of course, the drag on a fast-sinking fly-line is one of the reasons why many anglers prefer spinning with monofilament at this time of year. The spinning line has little water-flow resistance and thus less line drag; this enables depth and a slow speed to be obtained readily and together.

The statement that spinning in the spring is easy, may bring the response—'Why fish the fly at all at this time of year?' To which the answer can only be 'Because I prefer the method' or 'It is a requirement of the fishery rules'. But back to the fly and hooking the fish.

When I was a schoolboy I span for pike in winter on the river Nene in Northamptonshire. By January the weeds had been killed off by frost, the river often ran clear and the pike were in peak condition. I did not own a spinning rod but used the bottom two sections of a fly-rod, spinning off the line guide immediately below the top ferrule. A centre pin reel, flax line, spiral lead and a jointed wooden plug made up the outfit. A pike rarely took visibly; the line just stopped. Just like that. No snapping, clashing jaws, no hysterical thrashing, just a solid stop, as though the bait had hooked onto a sodden, sunken feather pillow. And so it is, usually, at the moment a salmon takes a sunk fly — and then he shakes his head. You have to decide on your next move after raising the rod to drive in the hooks. I will discuss the subsequent steps in the section on playing salmon.

There are fly fishermen of skill who say they are able to distinguish the exact moment when a salmon takes the fly into its mouth by the draw on a sunk line. At this moment they drop the point of the rod, let go a yard or two of line, which is swept down by the current below the fish, and then pull the hook into the corner, or scissors, of the salmon's mouth, when, they claim, a firm hold is almost invariably achieved.

I cannot say that this is my experience. I am of the 'pull back' school of thought — in other words if I feel anything at all I raise my rod, and if a salmon is there tighten into him. This is not a *strike*. No one should raise the rod violently in a *strike* — just a firm raising, whilst the line is gripped, to dig home the hooks.

This 'pull back' should not suggest a lack of sensitivity, far from it; fish with the line lightly held between the fingers of the free hand and you will detect those mere touches that a salmon can impart. These touches are as though a leaf, being swept downstream, had brushed the fly - these leaves may be a salmon! If this happens the salmon will often jump after touching the fly — even if he has not been pricked, as will not have happened in 'leaf touching'. Leave him for ten minutes, after which he may come firmly.

The first time I recall the leaf touch was on 9 March 1968 on the Welsh Dee at a water temperature of 40°F with the air at 50°F. The fly was a 2/0 Thunder & Lightning on a floating line (I did not then possess a sinker). He came again strongly, was hooked, and ran away upstream past me, but the hook came away after ten minutes. So much for large singles! On another occasion on 29 April 1972 I again felt the 'leaf touch', and the salmon then jumped to confirm his presence. It took half an hour to obtain a firm take from this fish of 12 lb, which is recorded in my diary as having jumped seven times when hooked, including a leap onto the far bank from which I was able to pull it back into the water together with a few whisps of grass on the leader. The fly this time was a No. 4 Thunder & Lightning.

One of the most telling assets an angler may have in sunk-line fishing is a knowledge of the bed rock, its contours, and where there are boulders and other obstructions to the flow which may make a comfortable lie for a salmon. This knowledge will be acquired over a number of seasons and is helped by inspection of the river in summer when the water is low — perhaps when sea trout fishing. If you do not have this knowledge seek out the services of a gillie who does.

It is a mistake to fish many rivers, searching always for a better water which seethes with eager fish — you are unlikely to find such a place unless you have all the time in the world and a considerable personal fortune. It is much better to learn one or two beats on a couple of rivers really well — it takes years to do this, for salmon lies alter as the water rises and falls, and new information will be gained each season. The local angler generally owes his success to river knowledge rather than any remarkable skill in casting.

Where should you fish in the pools at this time of year? This depends on the water height; salmon are lethargic in cold water and tend to be in deep places towards the quieter tails of the pools rather than the faster flowing necks which will be favoured in summer. In a heavy spate they may be just under the bank being unlikely to expend energy holding a mid-stream position against the strong flow of the current.

What time of the day is likely to be the most productive in March and the first half of April? My own preference is for the afternoon and evening. Fish will be caught in the morning, but on the whole tea-time is better, and the evening if it is warm. It all depends on the relative temperatures of the air and the water — the air must be above the river temperature to give the best chance.

If you arrive at the water at 10 am in March to find the air 50°F and the river at 43°F, then the day is full of promise. The river temperature may rise by 2° during the day, and such a rise may stimulate salmon to come on the take. The increase in water temperature will usually be indicated at this time of year by a hatch of large dark olives. When these flies drift up or down the valley on a soft breeze you know the time has come to make the greatest effort. I have also noticed in my still-water trout fishing in early April, usually with a sinking fly-line that the afternoon is more productive than the morning and I am not at all worried if fish are not taken before lunch. But the key to this is the air temperature — it must be above the water. But *must, never* and *always* are unwise words to use in salmon fishing, which is a sport in which the most unlikely events occur, and thus salmon are, occasionally, caught on the bitterest of days.

Floating line

Fly manipulation

In warm water, above 50°F, salmon will rise from their lies to take a fly just below the surface of the river. The fly may be fished on a floating line, but the leader must be under the surface. The floating line will thus come into use in April, probably the first half of the month in the South of England and the second half in Scotland. It is then likely to be the most effective line on which to catch salmon for the remainder of the season, unless the open season continues into November and December when the sunk line will again be required.

The method is not only effective but more exciting and easier to manage than sunk-line fishing. The fly may be cast up and across the river, across at right angles or down and across; following which it will be fished back in various ways until it hangs below the angler 'on the dangle'. The speed of retrieve will be governed by the necessity to keep the fly travelling to give it life. Thus on fast water little retrieving will be required because the current provides enticing movement, whilst in the slower, wider tails of pools a faster line movement must be instigated by the angler.

Consider first the 45° down and across throw. The angler casts his line at 45° down, out and across the river; following this the fly is returned to his side by the current pressing on the belly of the line until the line has straightened and the fly hangs below him. He then casts again, having, perhaps, moved a pace or two downstream. In these casts should an upstream mend be made in the line? The purpose of an upstream mend is to slow down the passage of the fly across the river — if this is desirable. After the cast has been made, mending is accomplished with the rod remaining in the horizontal, end-of-cast position, by lifting the line off the water, over and upstream, without moving the fly. In practice the final yard or two of line is not lifted, but left on the water as a short anchor so that the fly is not pulled.

A mend is required when a fast water is being fished across in order to take out, or prevent the formation of, the downstream belly which would otherwise form in the line and drag the fly rapidly across the water instead of trotting back to the angler at a speed which he is able to control. The fish, static on a lie, thus has time to be enticed by the fly, which is kept alive by the twists, lifts and vagaries of the current. Without a mend, a lightweight fly fished on a floating line might skid across the surface of a fast water, which is to be avoided.

A mend is not always required in a 45° downstream cast, for it is not necessarily correct for the angler to throw a line of a length requiring one, with perhaps second and third mends on the same throw. The short cast, to fish a lie close to the angler's bank, will not need mending. In the narrow fast neck of a pool, where salmon will be found in low water, neither mending nor retrieving is required — just a short 'down and across' cast, whilst the angler kneels or holds back from the bank to keep out of sight. The further down a pool one progresses the less mending will be needed if the current slows.

After the neck and middle, three further stages in the angler's progress down a pool of good length are likely to be met, each entailing a change in fly manipulation. The first is where your throw, after completing the down and across section, is made straight out at 90° to the bank and is then swept across by the current. The second is when the 90° cast is made, swept by the current and retrieved by hand to add to the waning power of the river. Finally, you could make the throw slightly upstream and across — and then retrieve as well. In a nutshell these variations slow the fly at the top of a pool and speed it up at the bottom.

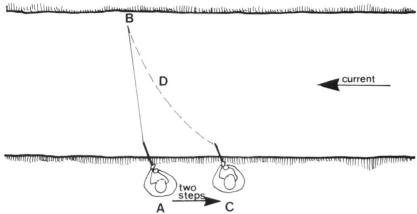

78 *Backing up the fly. Angler at A casts straight across to B in the wide slow tail of a pool. He then takes two steps upstream to C retrieving line at the same time. The fly and line will come across in the fast curve D. Repeat up the pool.*

Having arrived at the tail of the pool, the angler may then continue down the valley or fish back up the pool he has just covered, but this time starting at the tail. Not unnaturally this action is known as *backing up*. In this the cast is made across at 90°, the angler then takes two or three steps *upstream*, stripping in as he goes.

Backing up is a fast movement of the fly, combining current, hand retrieve and drawing from a position up the river — the fly whips across! Don't worry that it may be too fast for the fish - a determined salmon will have no difficulty in catching a rapidly-moved lure. *Backing up* enhances the surprise stimulus; the fly suddenly appearing from behind the salmon and being seen for the first time in the immediate taking area of the fish. This surprise is lost if the caster progresses slowly down the pool, for the fish will see the fly many times before it arrives in the taking area.

There is much to be said for starting at the tail of a pool and *backing up* the first time over, provided there is plenty of water in the river, or other cover, so that the angler is unlikely to be seen. The risk one takes is that the cast is made when opposite or just above the fish; this clearly puts the angler in a position where he is more likely to scare the salmon by his silhouette than if he had fished down on it with long casts whilst holding back himself.

Whilst on the subject of surprise; an angler would do better to fish down a pool rapidly with few casts, wait five minutes and then cover the same water again, perhaps with a change of fly, than go down once taking twice as much time and double the number of casts. For the angler who knows his river well and the exact position of a lie, there is little point in fishing down a pool until that place is reached. It is far better to make the first cast exactly where the fish is known to take. Surprise is then absolute. The first cast will wake him up and he will very likely take the second. If he is not at home the whole pool may then be fished. The desirability of a change in the speed of fly movement should be constantly in the mind of an alert fisherman. Each pool needs different speeds in different places within the pool, and the salmon at times respond to a change to a pace that would normally be acceptable.

I recall a recent June morning when I fished down a stretch of water with Black Dart flies at the retrieve speeds normally needed to bring results. By lunchtime I had risen seven salmon, but not one had touched the fly. Flies of 1 in., $1\frac{1}{4}$ in. and $1\frac{1}{2}$ in. had been tried — all were seen, acknowledged, but rejected after inspection. In the afternoon I changed a losing game by starting at the bottom of each pool and *backing up* without first fishing down in the conventional down and across manner. This action produced two surging high speed rises and two 10 lb salmon. There was no time for the fish to inspect and reject — just time to grab. Speed can be very helpful. I cannot produce an explanation of the earlier rejections, but the experience does underline the necessity of not continuing to fish in an unsuccessful manner.

A fast water speed may cause a lightweight fly to skate across the surface on its passage over the river. This is undesirable in most, but not all, situations. It is also almost fatal to success for the leader to float on top of the water, but this condition is readily solved by rubbing down the nylon with a wet cloth impregnated with Fuller's Earth and a few drops of washing-up liquid. If this is not available use mud, earth wetted in the river or soggy peat, these natural materials, however, are abrasive, may scratch the nylon and thus render it more visible. To keep the fly down either use a heavier type, such as the Copper Dart, or fish the fly of your choice off a sink-tip line.

A skidding fly is sometimes useful because it is a great attractor as it breaks the surface film. This is the basis of the dropper, trickled over the surface; the dropper may not be taken, though salmon sometimes come up and then take the tail fly. (But the risk of snagging whilst playing a fish on a leader with two flies has already been discussed.) A skidding fly may be a great raiser of salmon in a high wind. I first realized this many years ago when a gale whipped my fly up to the surface where it scuttled fast across the pool with the line billowing in the gusty wind. For some yards it was followed by a large open mouth which never quite caught up. The whole event was out of my control, but from time to time I now fish my single fly in this way at the narrow neck of a pool.

Size of fly
Size of fly is of great importance in all conditions and sparse dressing is particularly necessary in low water. A spate river is usually only fished in spate when tubes of 1–$1\frac{1}{2}$ in. are appropriate to the colour and volume of water, except in the final stages when the water is almost back to low; then a smaller fly might be tried for the last few hours. If in doubt as to fly size err on the side of a small sparse lure. Salmon have very good eyesight, even in coloured water.

Rivers usually rise rapidly in a spate, and whilst the angler may tie on a 1 in. fly as the rise commences, a $1\frac{1}{2}$ in. tube may be needed within the hour. This length would be fished throughout the high flood, when the angler should concentrate his effort on the sides of runs and the pool tails. A $1\frac{1}{4}$ in. tube should be the next step down during the period we might call the 'clearing and falling day', to be followed by the 1 in., and then perhaps a No. 10 or No. 12 Esmond-Drury-hooked Stoat's Tail in the final stages.

Those rivers not having great disparity in water levels, i.e. those that are spring-fed, require local knowledge of fly size. A No. 6 or No. 8, single-hooked, low water, finely dressed Hairy Mary might be the gillie's first choice in low clear waters in the north of Scotland. In fact my first five salmon on fly were on the Hairy Mary in those sizes in June 1959 on the Helmsdale. The same fly used in Hampshire on the Test, again in clear water will not do at all — a No. 4 Thunder & Lightning is much more likely to bring success, or a Silver Doctor of the same size on a bright day when the July and August grilse are about. This is supported by the diary entry of 10 August 1975.

> *River Test. Beat 1. Started 10 am with a number of fish showing and Tony rose two in Long Reach. I took 11 am 6 lb, noon 7 lb, and 12.30 pm 7 lb. All in run between Oak Tree and Kendle's Corner. Fly was one of Tony's Silver Doctors in size No. 4. All netted. Water temperature 68°F. Fish showed no interest in No. 6 Silver Doctor. Had lunch and drove home. After I left Frances lost a cow hooked on back cast. Tony lost a fish in Black Dog and Bernard took two fish in Long Reach of 8 lb each on prawn.*

Of particular interest is the large size of fly in so high a water temperature when fished on a floating line.

Salmon that rise but do not take

There are a number of ways of dealing with the fish that rises but does not take. The first is an alteration in the manner of fishing the fly that has induced the rise. Speeding up this fly, even to the extent of casting it higher upstream and then fishing it down fast before a final whip around above the lie may bring a take. It is also sensible to alter the direction of the fly's swim from towards, to away from the angler's bank. If the salmon rises at the limit of casting range such an alteration can be made by crossing to the other bank — if this is possible. Even if a long walk is entailed it may be rewarded: many times success has followed a change of bank.

I recall rising a salmon in June 1960 from the left bank in the sandy tail of a pool. I crossed to the other bank, cast out and again the fish rolled at the fly. Once more I walked several hundred yards upstream, crossed over, came down on the left bank from which I then hooked and landed the fish. The fly was a Hairy Mary, but my diary does not record the size — the salmon weighed 7 lb.

Such an alteration may result in casting from the shallow side into the deep water over which one was previously standing — it is usually preferable in any event to fish from shallow into deep rather than vice versa, for the angler may be visible on the bank above the lie of the fish. Direction of fly swim may be temporarily altered away from the angler by mending towards the far bank; this will be enhanced if the angler is able to wade out or wade out further than before.

Alteration of fly size and type should be tried, although it is my experience that a fish that has risen, if ultimately caught, will usually fall to the first fly to which it responded. Nevertheless, changes should be tried. The first action should be an alteration in pattern, for example Black Dart to Hairy Mary. The second to a smaller fly, and then a larger one before returning to the original. Each change should include a period of rest for the salmon — when I smoked cigarettes I would have one before giving the new offering a swim — a rest reintroduces surprise. It has been written that if one persists at a fish for an hour or more it may ultimately take, if not frightened, and that resting the salmon is not necessary. Rest or not, it is up to the individual to decide whether he is prepared to spend a valuable hour of prime fishing time on one salmon or go for another. Personally, I will continue at an individual salmon for as long as it responds — but if it does not come up after 20 minutes of work with different flies I move on and bear him in mind for a possible return at a later hour.

Weather and time of day

Weather conditions and time of day are inter-related and have a great bearing on results. Wind is very helpful — particularly an upstream gale, which makes the catching of salmon possible in low water. When great waves roll up the river through a deep wide pool, cast over to the far bank in a long throw and strip in fast. Fly size does not greatly matter, but a large fly is better than a small one. Salmon will come up in a curve at high speed — an action which often shows the dorsal fin. Such fish usually take with determination and are well-hooked in the scissors as they go down with the fly; there is no problem of when to raise the rod, for astonishment at the speed of the whole movement will overcome all thoughts of tightening until after the salmon has hooked himself and done the job for you.

Clear water and bright sunshine are not a happy combination, particularly if the sun shines down the river, for the floating line will throw a shadow on the river bed and this shadow precedes the line — the fish thus has advance warning of approach. A long leader helps, but it is better to return to fish these stretches when the sun has fallen or is hidden by cloud. I recall 26 April 1965 from my diary.

Tail of Wide Pool. Sunny and a few clouds. Rose a salmon three times to No. 6 Hairy Mary. Waited between casts for cloud to cover sun and intermittent breeze to ripple surface. Water medium/low; 8 lb.

and again on 29 September 1982.

As I waited in the car at 6.30 pm to come home Adrian hooked a fish of 10½ lb in the first stickle above Concrete Post. His shouts brought me with the net. One inch Copper Dart. We had fished over the stickle an hour earlier; in the meantime the sun came off the water, dropping behind the hills.

Time of day in June, July and August is particularly important in bright conditions, for in mid-summer it may be best to fish before the sun comes up, or after it has gone down. Dawn is not too soon nor dusk too late — far from it, these are the best times. In substantiation of an early start consider the diary record of 20 July 1980.

7.15 am, 7 lb; 8.15 am, 9 lb; 9.15 am, 9 lb. The first two on a 1¼ in. Black Dart tube fly. The third fish rose to the same fly but missed. Rested the fish for ten minutes then put on a 1¼ in. Hairy Mary which it took. All netted.

The diary does not mention that the sun then came out through the early white mist, burned the dew off the grass and, although I fished for the remainder of the day, not another salmon rose or was seen.

What are ideal floating-line weather conditions? If your polaroids steam up and the midges bite your wrists and ears, a salmon is likely to be yours if the river is in good order, for a dull humid day is excellent. Of all conditions a warm day of gentle rain is best, and if the rain continues for long enough it may cause the river to rise an inch whilst you are fishing, and this keeps salmon on the take. After a heavy shower immediately fish those good lies that earlier seemed to be without an occupant. Do not fish during a thunderstorm with a carbon fibre rod in your hand for this acts as a lightning conductor: fish when the storm has passed — it is a very good moment.

Salmon fishing is unpredictable, and successful fishing holidays lie in the laps of those gods who control wind, rain and water levels. I recall from my diary 24 October 1979 on the Deveron not far from Banff.

C.R.B. Upper Shaws. 8 lb. Black Dart (1 in.) at 10 am.
Bill. Middle Shaws. 14 lb. No. 4 Stoat's Tail at 11.30 am.
Bill. King Edward's burn. 4 lb. No. 4 Stoat's Tail. 3.00 pm.
C.R.B. Maggie mill. 16 lb. Black Dart (1 in.) at 4.00 pm.

The diary continues:

A wonderful day with the fly. Rose three more fish, with pulls from two of them. Netted all the large fish. Those spinning on opposite bank of lower beat had nothing! Bill's fly

was not, strictly speaking, a Stoat's Tail. It was a No. 4 Low Water double, tied mainly in black with a stoat's tail wing on top, black body ribbed gold, and blue and orange throat hackle. There were a few red hairs in with the wing.

The day before we had nothing in a cold dry wind but the water was falling after earlier rain. On 24 October it was mild. At the close of this splendid day it began to rain heavily and this continued for several hours; the river rose and not a fish was taken in the next six days.

Stealth

The stealthy care with which a salmon angler conducts his progress along the river will have a bearing on his catches. The colour of clothes may have little impact on the salmon but they are an obvious sign of a fisherman's determination to be unobtrusive. The angler unsympathetic to his situation and whose clothes stand out like a sore thumb will probably disturb not only the scene but the river as well, because it has not occurred to him that stealth is essential. His whole attitude is wrong. Don't bump about on the bank, or thump the river bed with studded waders, or use a clattering wading staff; fish cannot hear, but they are very sensitive to vibration. A scared salmon just melts away — one moment he is visible, the next, gone.

So far as is possible keep out of sight. A salmon cannot see in the angle of 12° immediately above the water surface, and you are thus probably invisible if wading with rocks between you and the fish. When standing on the bank you are visible, so take advantage of any cover by fishing from behind a bush or keeping back from the river edge. If you

79 *Without doubt there are salmon in this pool.*

80 *The angler kneels to avoid making a silhouette against the sky. The netsman has sited himself unobtrusively.*

81 *Douglas Moir keeps low on the Lyd.* **82** *A salmon is not likely to be warned in advance by Dr Tom Owen.*

cannot fish from behind cover then fish in front of it, i.e. use a tree behind you to cut out your silhouette against the sky.

The first thing to draw my attention to an otherwise well-concealed angler is if his rod is waving on an overhead cast. The movement, flash and colour catch the eyes as readily as a bee is pulled to a colourful flower. I wish manufacturers would make dull unvarnished rods — they would too if anglers did not, to their own detriment, prefer varnished ones. If it were not so heavy in the lengths above 12 ft 6 in., an impregnated cane rod would be ideal for the angler wishing to blend into his surroundings. The rod is brown, unvarnished and impervious to water. I own three of them: 12 ft 6 in. ferruled, 12 ft ferruled and 12 ft spliced. This latter rod is light in weight for cane, bends throughout when playing a fish, requires no maintenance other than an occasional dab of varnish to the silk ring bindings, casts well and is altogether desirable.

Line colour has already been considered. False casting is another eye-catching action and should be kept to a minimum: a line flashing over water scares the fish. On the whole in salmon fishing with a double-handed rod it is unnecessary to false cast, for sufficient line may be raised into the back cast and shot on the forward throw to cover most requirements. If a false cast is necessary to give distance or a change in direction, keep the false cast shorter than the final throw when the remainder of the line off the reel will be shot. In this way the false cast will only be made over water that has already been fished.

Wear polarized spectacles, not dark ones but a pair which will let in as much light as possible. These glasses not only protect the eyes but enable you to see an interested fish turn deep below the fly — sometimes this movement is almost unnoticeable but is revealed through polaroids momentarily as a slight lightening of a water patch against the dark background of the river bed. Such a movement may be invisible to the naked eye, and an angler without these glasses may miss the chance of trying such a fish two or three times — perhaps with success.

Hooking

The moment of hooking is that second or two for which all salmon fishermen live. The first solid pull is the result of much thought, skill and effort, and a little luck as well. The playing and landing are secondary satisfactions, in fact exhausting the salmon may not be satisfactory at all when one has reached that stage in a fishing life when conservation and respect for the fish exceed the desire to add to the contents of the deep freeze. The actual hooking is the great achievement. How may it be accomplished? The inattentive angler or novice will probably just find himself attached to a salmon, not having seen the fish come or realized what is happening.

It is the attentive angler who needs to exercise his skill when a salmon rises to the fly. If the fly is visible, and the orange wing of the Dart flies usually is, it is often possible to see when the fish has taken the fly into its mouth. When this has happened and the fish has turned away, raise the rod and tighten into him. When you cannot see the fly, but know where it is from the line direction, it is useful to watch the line/leader junction knot, or needle knot, when a fish has risen. If this knot moves

1 Gilbert Warne, doyen of the upper Dart, fishing Coombe Weir.

2 Colonel Douglas Moir fishing his own water of the river Lyd.

3 *(above)* Landing a salmon from Caddaford Turn Pool on the river Dart.

4 *(below)* Jamie Fergusson, having netted an 8 lb salmon for Lara Bingham.

5 *(right)* Salmon flies: *(top row)* four Black Dart tube flies, left to right, two inches to one inch; the Prawn Fly; Hairy Mary; Copper Dart. *(Bottom row)* Shrimp Fly; Stoat's Tail; Black & Orange Fly.

6 *(below)* Salmon baits: *(top row left to right)* Mepps Aglia Long—Copper; Mepps Aglia Regular—Gold; *(and on the right)* hook replacement. *(Second row)* standard Toby; 2 in. Blue & Silver Spey Devon minnow; *(right)* 2½ in. Yellow Belly Spey Devon minnow. *(Bottom row)* Rapala; a Flopy Plug.

7 Sea trout flies: *(top row, left to right),* 1 in. Silver Stoat's Tail; 1 in. Alexandra tube fly. *(Second row, left to right)* No. 4 Teal & Silver Blue; No 8 Black Lure. *(Third row, left to right)* Loch Ordie, Tony Allen Bucktail mayfly. *(Bottom row)* a homemade copper pike spoon for catching salmon.

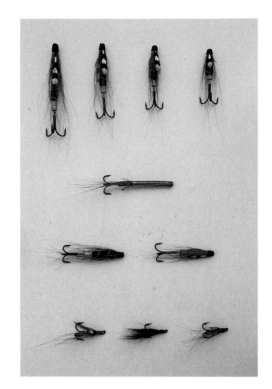

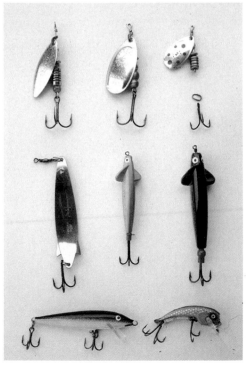

8 The Fhorsa, Isle of Lewis, an excellent location for salmon.

9 The River Test at the Broadlands Estate. Head river keeper Bernard Aldridge netting a salmon from Blackpool Pier at the lower end of Rookery Beat.

off raise the rod at once because the fish surely has the fly.

The point on which authorities disagree on hooking boils down to timing — when to raise the rod. If you cannot see either of the above indicators then wait until the fish has gone down before feeling for him: if he has the fly all will be well, if he has just passed by you will not have created disturbance by rod or line movement when he was close and may try him again.

The most difficult fish to hook is the one which takes when the fly is directly downstream of the angler on the dangle; in this situation it is easy for the salmon to be lip-hooked or for the fly to be pulled out of its mouth. On a short line when a fish comes up to the fly on the dangle the angler will probably see the mouth open, for the edges will appear white, the head then goes down but the fish may still be facing upstream, intending to sink back to the lie without turning. In order to do this the fish will momentarily have its head lower than the tail as the current presses down on the back of the head. In this head down position the angler will have a better chance of hooking the salmon than if he reacts by tightening at the sight of the open mouth.

It is very difficult to exercise sufficient control, to wait, but the necessity of control will be less if the rod is held high as the fly comes onto the dangle. There will then be a curve of line which will be straightened by the fish as its head drops. The pause whilst the straightening takes place is just sufficient to allow the turn down of the head. The easiest fish to hook is the one which takes when a long line is being fished — an argument in favour of a long cast down and across rather than fishing

closer to the angler. This closer water will already have been fished on earlier long casts.

It may be possible to cover the river with a short cast, made more across, but with a long one the angler is less visible, being further from the salmon. In addition, the curve in the line will allow the fish to turn before the line straightens and, with every chance of the hook being pulled into the scissors, the salmon should be firmly hooked. To sum up on hooking the visibly-risen fish: ignore it. You will hook more this way than by taking an active part, particularly if you have little experience. Start the day by saying to yourself 'I will do nothing if a fish comes to my fly'. Repeat this incantation at the head of each pool!

Line greasing

Now an explanation on line greasing and the fishing method known as the greased-line technique. The system of fishing is no different from the floating methods used today. In the past, grease was used to make fly-lines float. Do not put solid floatants onto a modern plastic-coated line because it is likely to cause damage. The coat will crack, and the line will then sink as the water seeps into the central core. A modern floating line floats because it is lighter than water. Additional floatants will not make it float better. Greasing the line dates to the period pre-1960. Lines were then made of silk and greased daily, or two or three times a day to make them float. Such lines were thinner for their weight than modern equivalents and they cast very well, but the grease always found its way onto the leader, which had to be constantly cleaned to make it sink. In those days it was not advisable to put your rod together at home, run the line through the rod rings, grease the line, attach the leader and then hook the fly under the reel mount. If the rod was carried thus by hand, or on the clips on the car roof, the grease on the line rubbed onto the leader that lay parallel along the rod length. On arrival at the river the leader had to be degreased before one started to fish.

5 Playing the salmon

Fly and spinning rods

At that moment when the rod tip bends over in an arc something alive is on the other end of the line that is jerking in small tugs: the salmon is shaking its head. Very startling; your first salmon. Surprise must not freeze the mind: your response should be immediate — a good firm lifting of the rod to thump in the hooks. It is best to have this over at once, despite the fear that the hooks may come away, because you will not increase the salmon's surprise by a strong pull at this stage. A hearty pull made later would be a different matter, possibly provoking an unexpected response. Right now he is trying to sort out what has hit him. If he is to be lost by an insecure hook hold, then the moment after the take is the best time to part company.

If wading, regain the bank at once whilst allowing line to run off the reel freely: without much pressure being exerted, the salmon will probably remain where he is or even move upstream. Until you are on the bank any action open to you in response to activity by the fish is very limited. Once on the bank you have freedom of movement.

Set out your aim: you are trying to tire the fish as rapidly as possible, consistant with a lack of *aerial gymnastics* on his part. Avoid stirring the sal-mon to frenzied activity; constant leaping is usually the result of mishandling by the angler, and every leap is dangerous. Aim to subdue him by solid slogging hard work — on his part. If the fish is hooked in the top or middle of a pool move down opposite to him. If he takes the lure close to the tail, or run off, then he must be persuaded upstream until he is in a safer place in the middle or at the top of a pool.

Always try to keep a salmon opposite or above you. The fish which is downstream of the angler has a number of advantages: he can sit on the current, which will balance out the pull of the line; he is closer to the tail of the pool and this direction is his most likely line of escape if mishandled; his mouth faces upstream, which increases the chance of the hooks being pulled out. So, keep opposite or below the fish and *out of sight*. When hooked a salmon has no idea what has happened: don't let him find out whilst he is still strong. A salmon that has seen his adversary will probably make a bolt for it, which may take him down and out of the pool, so *keep out of sight*. If you are on the bank, having hooked the fish in the middle of the pool downstream of you, move downriver until opposite or slightly below the fish. Then, whilst hidden from him, on your knees if necessary or behind a bush in a little river, keep a

83   *The salmon splashing in the bottom*   **84**   *and turned to the netsman.*
right-hand   corner   must   be   brought
upstream...

85 *The netsman engulfs the fish, sup-porting the net at the shaft junction.*

86 *The fish is killed with the 'priest', and the fly removed for further use. The rod on the left is in danger of being trodden on.*

87 *An 8-pounder nears the end of a* **88** *The fish continues to fight.*
fight with Lara Bingham. Netsman Jamie
Ferguson waits with net submerged.

89   *The salmon has been drawn over the submerged net, which is now raised...*

90   *and pulled to the rock. It would be safer if the fish had been netted head first but why grumble....*

91   *All hands help...*

92   *safe at last.*

93 *Hooking a salmon; the bush behind*   **94** *Where is he?*
prevents silhouette.

95   *The fish is being drawn upstream to the net. This is dangerous as the leader is first to meet the net ring, but there was no choice in this particular circumstance. Note leverage provided by butt of double-handed rod inside left thigh.*

96   *Hand at net ring to lift ashore.*

97 *The fish is killed at once. The priest is carried in the pocket with a cord about the neck.*

steady pressure on the fish with the rod at right angles to the bank and projecting as far out over him as is possible.

Stay like this, if he will let you, and he probably will, for at least five minutes with a fish of about 10 lb. His nose will be on the bottom but he will be forced to work to counteract your upward pull — some of the steam will have been taken out of him at the end of this period and he will be potentially less dangerous. Now is the time to stir him up a bit — not too much — by altering the direction of pull. Dropping the rod point slightly and drawing towards your bank will cause the salmon to head upstream and out towards the other bank, the current will then press on his flank and, like a lemon pip, he will be squeezed out, up and away. Now raise the rod again and, being upstream, he

will have to fight the current and the rod.

This may be done two or three times, for a salmon will often keep returning to the same place in the pool — no doubt the current suits him in that spot. Sooner or later if he has weight, say over 7 lb, he will try to escape by making an upstream or downstream run. Upstream is no problem; he will not go far unless of portmanteaux dimensions. Downstream is another matter — we must do our best to stop him by guile. In heavy water it is not possible to stop a 10 or 12 lb fish, let alone a 15 lb one, running out of the tail of a pool by brute force; at any rate it is not possible without the considerable risk that the hook will bend out or come away. You might succeed if the hook is well back inside the mouth on 15 lb test nylon because there would be a straight pull on the hook, or hooks if using a treble or double. But if the salmon is held by a single, fine wire at the edge of the mouth, the strain on the bend of the shank is immense and the gape will probably open, losing you the fish.

There is an alternative to brute force: the method is successful in four cases out of five. *Before* the salmon is within 7 or 8 yd of the danger line drop your rod point, strip off a couple of pulls from the reel and let all go slack. The salmon will swing around to face upstream because he cannot breathe readily whilst facing down river; you may then tighten gently and walk him up away from danger. It takes courage, letting all go slack, but almost always works if done in time, but it will not work if left too late when the fish is in the suction draw between the rocks leading to the next pool. 'Walking up', referred to above, is simple: hold the rod over the river at right angles to the bank, exert a steady upstream pull on the fish, which will usually follow, sliding through the water in as smooth and streamlined a passage as a gondola in a Venetian canal.

The correct course of action when a salmon jumps will always be debatable. Personally, I drop the rod point because I think that aerial action is more violent than underwater movement, which is damped down by the displacement of water. A tail thrashes and a body twists dramatically in the air, transmitting jerks on the hook hold. Other than with grilse, which can jump without warning, (the netsmen at the river mouth call them hoppers) a salmon gives a couple of seconds notice of his intention to jump by a violent acceleration, which builds up momentum for the leap. This speeding up should warn the angler to be ready to drop his rod point, thus slackening the line.

Slack line is risky and worrying; it is always a relief to raise the rod, tighten, and find him there: but to hold on tight throughout the leap is a greater risk. When playing a salmon the angler should have in mind throughout the battle the place in which he intends to land the fish by beaching, tailing or using the net. Let such a place, if possible, be up the pool away from the run-off, for an exhausted heavy salmon swept away downstream past the landing place is very difficult to recover. Try not to net a fish in fast water: it is difficult to hold the open net against the flow, which will pull on the meshes of the bag, and the current will give guidance and help to the salmon. Try for a slack bay or an area of back current where the fish will lose direction; such a harbour may be only a 4 or 5 yd wide dent in the bank, but that is sufficient. When a fish starts to show the light colour of its flank or belly it is becoming tired, and the angler should make his move towards the slack area. The actual netting has already been described in Chapter 2.

The action to be taken if a salmon escapes downstream can only be decided in the particular circumstances. Entering the river to follow, if you cannot proceed along the bank because of a tree or other obstruction, is a decision for the individual and will depend upon the strength and depth of the water as well as the athletic ability of the fisherman. If I know the river intimately I will enter if I don't expect to exceed a depth above my waist or be swept away — remember to remove your wallet from your hip pocket first! If in doubt as to safety then don't risk yourself — it may be possible with good tackle to inch the fish slowly back by hand lining. Very occasionally a salmon will be lost downstream through no fault of the angler — it is better to accept this than to endanger yourself and others who might come to your rescue.

Although these suggestions have been written with fly-fishing in mind as the principal method they apply equally to spinning, but with one or two differences owing to the equipment. The spinning rod is likely to be shorter than the fly-rod, and this lack of reach makes it more difficult to execute manoeuvres which avoid obstructions in the river and on the bank. At the same time the spinning outfit has one or two advantages over the fly equipment. In those situations where slack line is given to a salmon to persuade it not to run out of the tail of a pool the giving of line, which amounts to removing any pull on the fish, is readily accomplished on a fixed spool reel by opening the bail arm. When the salmon has faced upstream the reel handle may be turned, the bail arm will swing over, pick up the monofilament line and pressure may be resumed. With the multiplier the check may be taken off momentarily to accomplish the same result. These actions are not possible with most fly reels. A further advantage will accrue in

the strength of the outfit: a stiff rod and nylon that tends to be a few pounds heavier than the fly leader. These give the angler a greater chance of successfully pumping up an exhausted fish that has been washed downstream.

'Walking up', referred to earlier in this chapter is applicable to both fly and spinning rods. At times a fish will refuse to co-operate more than once, but the following fishing diary extract of 25 May 1967 records the movement of a very acquiescent salmon:

Heavy rain previous day and overnight. River running strong but clear 8 am. Fished until 3 pm, water dropped 6 in. Took fish 11½ lb on No. 6 Thunder & Lightning in pool above bridge. Fish went down through bridge three times, and each time I was able to walk it up. Had fished this pool at 10 am without result until the water warmed up and dropped. At 4 pm took 7½ lb, No. 6 T & L at top of Splay Pool on left side. Fish hooked itself on fly that trailed unattended in water as I jumped back across the stepping stones.

The second salmon can only be described as helpful!

6 Spinning

I caught my first salmon in the river Findhorn in Morayshire in 1954. It came on a Devon minnow in high-coloured water from the pool called Craigie on Darnaway. Luck played a part, in fact the major contribution came, without doubt from St Peter who must have looked down with sympathy out of a watery sky. The salmon helpfully attached itself, despite my amateur efforts with a Hardy's Elarex multiplying reel loaned by the Estate. As the head keeper said, 'that's one more than I expected'. His remark didn't deter me. Returning south from Scotland I went to Hardy's in Pall Mall to purchase a spinning rod and an Elarex. The reel, No. 475 according to the ticket in the original box, is still with me and in use. The Elarex has been out of production for some years and existing models will become valuable to the antique tackle collector and dealer.

Equipment

Rods

As suggested under fly equipment, a long rod is better than a short one. The same advantages will accrue to the holder of a spinning rod of good length in playing a salmon. As fly-fishing is much more enjoyable you only need to spin when conditions of river volume and temperature make this method the most likely course to bring results. Generally speaking, this means during the early spring and late autumn when large baits are needed. A little weight helps us to fish deep, and the spinning rod must be of sufficient power to cast leads of up to about $\frac{3}{4}$ oz and perhaps a metal bait in addition.

Glass fibre spinning rods should have the following throwing capacities:

8 ft 6 in. $- 1\frac{1}{4}$ oz
9 ft 6 in. $- 1\frac{1}{2}$ oz
10 ft 0 in. $- 1\frac{3}{4}$ oz.

There are also shorter rods, but 8 ft 6 in. is about the minimum for a general purpose salmon spinning rod. A rod of 9 ft 6 in. is much better and gives a reach advantage if the rod is also required for prawning with a paternoster (see p. 128, fig. 108), for which the 8 ft 6 in. model is rather short. Manufacturers seem to optimistically imagine that the arms of anglers grow in length to match the extended butts built on long rods. A long butt is an irritation, particularly when the rod has to be swapped from hand to hand across the tummy with each cast when using a right-hand wind multiplying reel. It may be that rod manufacturers are all slim men!

As spinning rods are, on the whole, just used to chuck out lumps of metal,

98 *The author's first salmon, 1954. River Findhorn in Morayshire, on Darnaway Castle estate.*

plastic and wood, without the finesse of fly presentation, there is no need to go to the expense of carbon fibre or split-cane. In fact the 8 ft 6 in. glass fibre model weighs 8 oz., which is only 1 oz. more than a carbon fibre rod of the same length. Spinning rods should have a large 1 in. diameter butt ring. A 9 ft Abu salmon spinning rod in my possession has a butt ring of $1\frac{5}{8}$ in. Do not buy a rod with a small diameter ring in this position or the coils of line coming off a fixed spool reel will be held up at this point. Impregnated cane spinning rods have all the power and durability required, but a 9 ft 3 in. model weighs about 14 oz. whilst a 9 ft 6 in. hollow

99 *Mitchell 300 A fixed spool reel on Hardy 8 ft 6 in. fibreglass, double-handed spinning rod. Monofilament line. The slipping clutch adjustment is at the front of the line spool.*

glass fibre rod only scales in the region of $11\frac{3}{4}$ oz. The split-cane costs considerably more.

Spinning reels
The types available and in general use are the fixed-spool reel and the multiplier. The former is the more versatile and the latter gives the angler greater control when playing a fish, but is limited in application to the casting of heavier spinning baits, and weighted worm and prawn tackle. It is easier to teach a person to spin with a fixed-spool reel for a number of reasons: one of these is that the rod may be held in the right hand during the cast and the retrieve. With the multiplier it is necessary to shift the rod to the left hand after the cast in order to wind the reel with the right hand.

The fixed-spool reel

One trade catalogue describes the Mitchell 300 as 'The most famous reel in the world.' Another dealer states in his description 'Possibly the most famous and best-selling of all Mitchell reels.' There is no doubt that this reel is very widely used and is ideal for salmon spinning in this country. It comes with two spools. The deeper spool has the greater capacity and should be filled with approximately 100 yd of pliable 18 lb test nylon monofilament: this is sufficient in strength and length for most situations. The shallow pool will hold about 80 yd of 8 lb test nylon, and this may be employed to spin a lightweight lure in summer for sea trout. The nylon should be filled to within $\frac{1}{10}$ in. of the spool lip. If overfilled, coils of nylon will come off the spool when casting and tangles will form. If underfilled it is not possible to cast any great distance.

When filling the reel from a spool of new nylon do not place the spool on a pencil and re-wind onto the reel, for each turn of the bail arm will add one twist to the nylon as it is wound on. Instead, place the spool flat on the ground, stand above and wind onto the reel. In this position it will be seen that when the spool is placed on the floor on one side many twists will form as the reel is wound, but if placed on the other side the spirals coming off the spool in one direction will be matched by opposite coils going onto the reel; in this manner twists are kept to a minimum. The correct side of the new nylon spool to be kept on top will become apparent as soon as winding begins.

Even if the reel is filled in this manner a number of twists will form when a new line is first used on the river. It is advisable to take these out before fishing. This may be done by threading the line through the rod rings and then attaching a Wye weight by the swivel (this would be the incorrect end when fishing). A few long casts downstream will allow any twists to come out; they will untwirl against the swivel in front of the lead.

The reel requires very little maintenance, but a daily drop of '3 in 1' oil on the bail arm return spring, the bearings at each end of the bail arm, and at the point where the shaft of the winding handle enters the housing, will ensure long life. Other than this, a few drops of oil once a year through the end screw will lubricate the internal complications. Before starting to fish, the drag-adjusting knob at the front of the spool should be set to give correct slipping clutch resistance against the pull of a salmon. If the drag is set too tight a fish may be lost when the reel fails to give line. If set too loose, insufficient pressure will be applied to the fish. For the novice assembling his outfit the correct drag may be set by hooking the bait to a tree or stump, raising the rod and applying increasing pressure until the reel slips at the pull judged to be correct.

There are three main advantages in the fixed-spool reel over the multiplier. The first is the ability to cast both light and heavy weights: this makes the reel suitable for heavy spring fishing and for casting the small baits used with little, if any, weight in summer. The second is that line tangles are infrequent, the reason being that if the bait in its flight through the air hits an obstruction then line ceases to be pulled from the static spool, which is not revolving. Sudden stoppage of the bait in mid-flight is the most common cause of tangles with revolving reels. Finally, a bait may be flicked out from a position under trees, or between them, where there is little room for a full swing cast.

The multiplier

Good quality multiplying reels are expensive, being almost twice the price of a fixed-spool reel of simple but sound design and construction. The multiplier usually has a gearing of three or four revolutions of the line drum to each turn of the handle, the line is wound level on the drum by a distributor which moves back and forth across the width of the revolving spool. When casting, the inertia of the drum filled with line has to be overcome by the weight of the bait — this will preclude the use of the

100 *Abu Ambassador multiplier spinning reel. The thumb on the spool acts as a sensitive brake when playing a salmon. Braided Dacron line.*

lightest baits required in summer. Once the inertia is overcome and the spool starts to revolve, a stage has been reached where energy is stored in the moving drum. If the bait then hits an obstruction, such as the branch of an overhanging tree and ceases to pull off line to match the unwinding drum, the reel will continue to revolve and a tangle will be created before the thumb can stop the reel. This tangle does not occur when the bait hits the water in the expected place, at the end of the cast, for small brakes inside the reel and pressure from the thumb on the spool will ensure the reel stops revolving as the bait alights. It is the unexpected stop, when the thumb is too late to apply brakage, that causes a tangle. The bait will slow down gradually at the end of the cast, without overrunning, if the built-in brake is correctly set before fishing. The brake should be adjusted

to allow the weight of the minnow or other lure, when suspended outside the rod tip, to pull line slowly off the reel.

Despite these drawbacks, the reel is a delight to use for heavy spinning in spring, and where there is plenty of room for a good swing in the cast. It is not so good at flicking out baits in confined circumstances where there is little room to swing the rod to build up momentum in the minnow. The great advantage in the reel is the infinitely variable pressure that may be applied to a salmon being played, by the thumb used as a brake upon the spool of line.

Lines for spinning reels
Between the end of the spinning line and the bait it is advisable to have a 1 yd nylon trace: a trace of greater length will be awkward to cast and is unnecessary. This nylon should be of a lesser strength than the reel line. As it is unwise to fish with nylon of less than 15 lb test this means that the reel line should be about 18 lb test. The advantage of a trace of lesser breaking strain than the reel line is apparent when it is caught on the bottom of the river or in a tree; the short trace will break and the reel line will usually be recovered intact. It is inconsiderate to other users of a river to leave 20 or 30 yd of reel line trailing from a bait caught on the river bed or suspended from an overhanging branch.

Monofilament should be used on the fixed-spool reel, and the 18 lb test ought to have a diameter of about 0.40 mm. The nylon must not be springy: buy the best quality supple line you can find, preferably in a light colour, which will show the position of the line above the water. Camouflaged nylons are very difficult to see against a dark river, you won't be able to follow the exact passage of the bait. The visibility of the mono-filament line will not scare fish, for the trace may be made of an unobtrusive brand.

A braided line should be used on a multiplying reel, being less liable to tangle. The best I have found is Mil-ward's Searanger: available in 150 yd spools at 20 lb test, and upwards, the 20 lb is very suitable for salmon spinning. This line is a non-stretch terylene polyester yarn, rot proof and of a very useful, light green colour.

Do not use small diameter low stretch nylon for the trace, which, attached to lead at one end and a bait at the other, is subject to sudden jerks and stress. The 15 lb suggested should have a diameter of not less than 0.37 mm.

Swivels and leads
It is advisable to have a swivel and some kind of anti-kink device at the junction of the line and the trace. The simplest system is to use a Wye lead: this has a wire loop at one end to which the reel line should be knotted; a swivel is at the end to which you attach the trace. The bait will then revolve on the swivel against the 'stop' of the lead. Be sure not to attach the line to the swivel or the revolving bait will twist the trace, the swivel being at the wrong end. Wye leads of $\frac{1}{4}$ oz., $\frac{1}{2}$ oz. and $\frac{3}{4}$ oz. should be carried. One precaution ought to be taken before fishing with the Wye — remove the spring clip, attached to the swivel by the manufacturers. This clip is for the easy attachment of an additional swivel, but the clip could open when playing a salmon. I remember a river keeper on the Hampshire Avon, where salmon run large, showing me a splayed-out clip on a Wye, which had resulted in someone losing a fish. Another

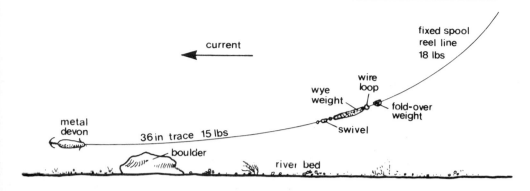

current

fixed spool
reel line
18 lbs

wire
loop

wye
weight

fold-over
weight

metal
devon

36 in trace 15 lbs

swivel

boulder

river bed

All knots tucked half bloods

current

wooden
devon

boulder

river bed

swivel

wye weight

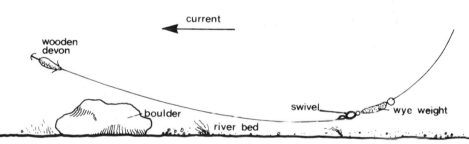

102 *Above   Making-up a spinning outfit.* Top *Position of components. The
metal Devon minnow will fish close to the
river bed and may snag on rocks unless the
angler knows their position.* Lower *A
wooden Devon will swim above the Wye
weight and thus clear obstructions.*

---

101 *Top left — Wye lead. Attach trace to
swivel — reel line to metal loop. The spring
clip on the swivel has been removed for
safety;* top right *fold-over lead;*
centre-top *BB swivel with reel line at one
end, trace at the other. Fine nylon leads
to Paternoster of American snap link
swivel and screw bomb weight;* bottom
*swivel heads and bombs of various
weights.*

method of joining the line to the trace
is to tie in a ball-bearing swivel with a
fold-over lead immediately above the
swivel; No. 2 fold-overs are ideal. Also,
if using a small Wye lead of perhaps
$\frac{1}{4}$ oz., carry two or three fold-overs in
your pocket; these additional weights
may then be added or removed to
achieve the required depth without your
having to re-tie two knots to change the
Wye. For a very fast revolving bait in
heavy water, a second swivel of the ball-
bearing type may be tied in half-way
along the trace.

Subsequent note on lead fishing weights
Recently, press reports have confirmed
that it will become illegal to sell lead
weights of sizes up to and including 1 oz.

From discussions with people in the tackle trade it appears that a Wye-shaped weight of a material other than lead may evolve. Even so, the new legislation will forbid the use of a new Wye in conjunction with lead 'fold-overs' as a ready means of increasing or reducing weight whilst fishing a pool. A new brass weight system is now on sale called the Screw Bomb, which is excellently engineered by Dexter Products of Great Britain. The system may be purchased in a set consisting of a threaded swivel head, into which are screwed the bombs of various weights from $\frac{1}{8}$ oz. to $1\frac{1}{2}$ oz. I suggest the best way of attaching the swivel head to the line is by using an American Snap swivel at the line/trace junction, being sure to knot the reel line to the snap link end of the swivel. This device, although less stream-lined than the Wye, has the great advantage that weights may be swiftly changed according to the depth and current, as you progress down a pool — you just screw in a different bomb.

Addendum: The Wye weight is now available in zinc, which being less dense, weighs slightly less than the former lead Wye in any given size.

Artificial spinning baits
These include Devon minnows, plugs, Tobies, Mepps, and their variables too numerous to mention. Almost all are equipped with treble hooks.

The Devon minnow—probably the most widely used spinning bait, as it is particularly well-suited to the heavy water of early spring, and the late autumn, when a large lure is needed. The stream-lined shape enables you to fish deep with it without great water resistance

dragging against the rod; this, with some spoon baits, makes the retrieving of each cast heavy, slow and tedious. The range of sizes required in February, March and April will be between 2 and $2\frac{1}{2}$ in. On some rivers a 3 in. minnow may be needed in cold heavy water, but on the whole a $2\frac{1}{2}$ in. will be fine. A 'showy' Devon is best in thick water after rain — the yellow and green Yellow Belly is probably the most popular. As the flow clears a change may be made to Brown & Gold or Black & Gold, and then as the river settles back it is worth trying a Blue & Silver. (The size of minnow will be discussed later.)

Devons are available in metal, plastic and wood. The metal type is heaviest, the most expensive and will really scratch the bottom of the river. For years I used metal exclusively and the results were good, but unless the contours of the riverbed are known in detail many minnows will snag and be lost. There is a particularly good brand of plastic Devon called the Spey: the body being just the right weight and with stream-lined fins it is almost indestructible. The Spey is considerably cheaper than a metal minnow. Many anglers use wooden Devons, following the supposition that they fish a little higher in the water than the lead at the line/trace junction, and thus will swim over obstructions. I cannot claim much success with wooden baits; the plastic fins joined to some types break readily, and the paint with which they are coloured tends to flake. Regardless of the material of which the Devon is made, the angler must pay careful attention to the mount

103 *Materials to make a Devon minnow mount.*

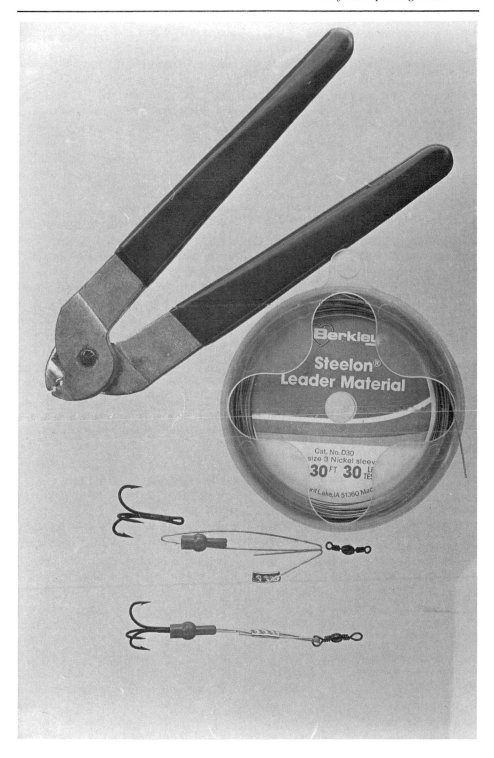

and the hooks: very few are of good quality — the worst are unbelievably bad, with soft eyeless hooks and single strands of twisted wire looped over the division between the three hooks of a treble.

The Spey comes with an excellent mount, but it is best to make your own if in any doubt. All you require is a spool of plastic-coated Berkley 30 lb test Steelon wire, No. 4 sleeves, No. 7 swivels, tulip beads and a No. 4 or No. 6 ringed treble code X1 by Partridge. Use a pair of crimping pliers to squeeze the sleeve tight on the wire. Tulip beads are not always easy to find: a friend who supplied me with a box wrote on the outside 'Take two after meals. Will cure anything.' Plastic-coated steel wire is a worthwhile refinement — the mount will not rust in your tackle box.

Having been fairly unenthusiastic about wooden Devon minnows, I recently rediscovered their possibilities. Standing by the river in October 1986, after the season had closen, I waited with a telephoto-lensed camera on a tripod: the intention being to obtain a picture of salmon jumping a weir during their autumn migration up-river on a spate. It was a tedious business, and frustrating too, for each salmon that leaped did so outside the narrow field of view afforded by the lens. There was a cold wind that numbed my finger held ready on the camera button. Herman Myhill, a keen and experienced fisherman, joined me and relieved my finger as I drank hot coffee. The conversation turned to salmon spinning and the start of the next season, and eventually the banning of Wye leads. Herman said that he preferred the wooden minnow because they fished a trifle higher in the water than the lead, and were less likely to be lost

as a result. When I asked him whether they were expensive to buy, he replied, 'Ah no, I make them all myself. Something to do in the winter.'

His craft demonstrates profound dedication and the distilled product of much experiment. He selects suitable hazel branches, cuts them and then dries the wood for one year. The dried stick is cut into suitable lengths: $1\frac{1}{2}$, 2, $2\frac{1}{2}$ in. and so on, and then drilled. Finally he shapes the minnow by hand to a slightly irregular curve and fits a pair of fins before applying two coats of aluminium paint, followed by a coat or two of the desired colour. The nylon trace is fed through the Devon and sits on a tulip bead before being tied directly to a treble hook. When a fish is hooked the minnow readily slides up the trace out of harms way, and a high percentage of the salmon which take are landed. Without doubt their device is successful, and the reason?

'Well Charles, no natural fish swims in a straight line in the manner of a lathe turned or metal Devon. Mine wobbles a little and deviates from the path of retrieve. That's natural.' — And indeed it is.

The Mepps—Of the many spoon baits available the Mepps type is probably the most widely used, particularly in late spring and in the summer. The No. 2 is a good size for downstream spinning — larger sizes cast down river have too much water resistance in fast places to be fished comfortably. The No. 3 and No. 4 have a place for upstream casting when the bait is spun downstream faster than the current. It is wise to regard the hooks of some spoons as suspect in the smaller sizes — I have lost salmon when the fine wires have bent out. If the hook of any spoon of this type is weak, cut it off, fit a Mustad No. 2 Type 9944 split oval ring and a ringed hook of good quality such as code X1 by Partridge. Various coloured Mepps may be purchased — the copper shade glints in an attractive manner.

104 Top Homemade copper pike spoon, much loved by salmon. middle *Toby with flying treble.* bottom *detail of flying treble with spur for toby.*

The Toby—This lure is taken by many salmon: it swims well and fishes deep in fast water. It may also be cast upstream in summer and reeled back faster than the current. The drawback to the bait is leverage by the long body on the hook hold: a higher percentage of fish will be lost due to the hooks working free than will be the case with the Devon and the Mepps. Losing fish on the Toby and spoons of similar design may be overcome: attach a length of 20 gauge stain-

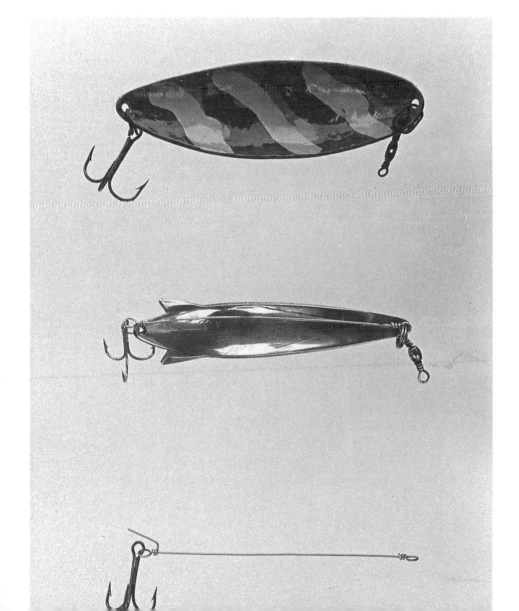

less wire to the top ring, at the other end of the wire, at the tail of the Toby, twist on a treble hook leaving a wire spur to be poked into the hole in the tail of the Toby; this spur will spring free when a fish takes, leaving the fish held on the flying treble. I first came across this arrangement on the river Teith, near Doune in Perthshire.

It is, of course, very easy to make your own curved spoon baits from a sheet of 16 gauge copper; the only tools you need are a pair of tin shears, a drill and a round-headed hammer. One side of such a bait may be polished to a dull gleam, and the other painted red with black or yellow stripes. Pike love them as well as salmon — in fact it is a job to keep salmon kelts away when pike spinning in the Dorset Stour in January and February.

The plug—The only plug I carry is the No. 1 red rubber Flopy, which is made in France. This little soft wobbling bait is a good attractor in the summer; it should be fished down and across to be retrieved 6 in. or a foot below the surface.

In conclusion: spinning baits are available in a great variety of colours, shapes and sizes. The angler who has a few Devons of $2-2\frac{1}{2}$ in. in length, No. 2 and No. 3 Mepps and a Flopy will be well-armed. Any additional ammunition will turn one into a heavily laden, rattling, travelling tackle stockist.

Spinning techniques

As with double- and single-handed fly casting there is no doubt that the best course to follow in learning to cast well with a spinning rod must be to have lessons from a professional instructor. An hour or two on the river bank under qualified tuition will enable the mechanics of casting with fixed spool reels to be mastered to a fair level of competence — the multiplier takes a little longer. I am not, therefore, going to describe how to throw a bait, but it is important to consider the flight path of the bait in the air as it travels across the river.

Basically there are two types of cast: the overhead and the swing. In the second method the rod tip performs a scooped curve, starting and finishing at points that are slightly higher than the dip towards the ground in the middle of the path of the rod tip. This scooped cast cannot be commenced if the trace is longer than one yard, for the starting point of the rod tip will be too high in order to prevent the minnow at the end of the trace resting on the ground. In the scooped swing cast the flight of the bait across the river will be flat and almost parallel to the water.

In the overhead cast the bait will rise in a curve into the air, reaching its high point about two-thirds of the way across the river. This upward path is likely to result in the novice propelling his bait up into the overhanging branches of trees on his side of the river or dropping the bait, as it falls, through the branches on the other side. Longer throws are possible with the overhead cast, which may be used on wide, open rivers, but if there are overhanging trees the scooped cast is safer.

105 *Dr Tom Owen with a 20 lb spring fish in March. Mitchell 300 reel. The bait was an old brass Hardy spoon.*

106 *Bunny and Joanna Bird with a 14-pounder. March. Mitchell 300. 2 in. Brown & Gold metal Devon minnow.*

If your bait does become entangled in a tree branch or rocks above water on the far bank, there is little you can do other than pull and break the trace: before you do this remember that nylon is elastic, the tree branch will bend and act as a catapult, the projectile is the weight or minnow and you are the target! In this dangerous situation adopt the following course: wrap a handkerchief around your hand and then two or three turns of line (your skin will not then be cut by the nylon), turn your back, put down your head and walk away until the trace snaps and the weight flies across the river. The weight is quite likely to be flattened at one end if it hits a rock on your bank — if it hits you on the bottom you will be bruised but you will have avoided being hit in the face! Remember to pull from the handkerchief-covered hand and not directly from the reel spool; this would result in the line cutting down into the coils on the drum.

The strength of 15 lb nylon is greater than many imagine. I once asked a friend, to whom I had given a spool of 15 lb Platil Strong for his salmon-fly leaders, whether he found the material satisfactory. 'Oh yes' he replied with a smile 'I've pulled quite a few fair-sized branches off the trees.'

Releasing the bait that has stuck below water level on the river-bed must also be considered. If spinning downstream, do not pull hard on the bait; this is only likely to jam it more securely. Instead, turn over the reel bail arm, or take your thumb off the spool of a multiplier, allow several yards of line to run off and form a loop downstream of the bait, close the reel and strike sharply; the pull from behind will often free the bait. If this does not work pull from different directions; if still unsuccessful I pull and break the trace. Some anglers endeavour to release stuck baits with an 'otter' — this is a length of stick, a bottle, or a plywood disc that is run down the line and worked out across the river to the bait, where its action above the snag may jiggle the hooks free. Such a device may be made on the river bank with a length of string and a piece of wood — I do not use them, however, in case the disturbance frightens the salmon.

The correct choice of spinning tac-

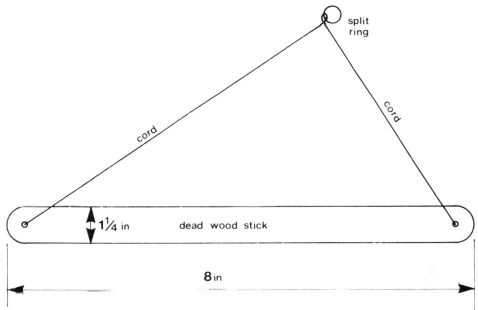

split
ring

cord

cord

1¼ in   dead wood stick

8 in

107   *The 'Otter'. May be constructed on the river bank from a short piece of dead tree branch and a length of baler twine.*

tics — downstream or upstream casting; fishing deep or near the surface; bait types, colours and sizes — largely depends on a combination of the natural conditions of water temperature, volume and clarity. These natural factors are, to a large extent, seasonal in their changes and important to understand.

Cold water spinning
Include in this category water temperatures below 50°F — these occur in spring up to about mid-April, and recur in the late autumn. During these weeks not only is the water likely to be cold but it will flow more heavily and be deeper than in the summer. At the same time, the salmon tend to hug the bottom and to be lethargic; thus a bait of good size, fished deep, is more likely to stir their chilled senses than a small lure travelling near the surface. The larger sizes of Mepps create too much water resistance when spun downstream in a strong flow; the best baits for these conditions are the Devon minnow, the Rapala and the Toby. These baits should be used at the fast, strong neck of the pool and down the main run. A No. 2 Mepps may be substituted when this water has been covered and the wide tail of the pool is reached.

Experience will enable you to choose the correct size of bait on arrival at the river: the combination of water temperature, colour and flow must all be considered when selecting the length and material of the bait and also the colour. Let us consider the following water conditions:

Water temperature 40°F, coloured, full flow. Use 2½ in. Yellow Belly Devon minnow, preferably metal.

Water temperature 44°F, some colour, medium flow. Use 2 in. Yellow Belly — preferably a lighter weight plastic Spey.

Water temperature 44°F, clear but full flow. Use 2 in. Blue & Silver metal Devon.

Water temperature 47°F, clear, medium flow. Use 1½ in. Blue & Silver metal Devon.

Water temperature 48°F, clear, low water. Use No. 2 Mepps.

In the above examples Yellow Belly and Blue & Silver Devons have been suggested: these will be effective in those rivers that run off agricultural land where rainfall turns the river a muddy brown, dropping back through a greenish hue, before becoming clear. The moment in such rivers after a flood when the water starts to change from brown to green signals the time to commence fishing. On rivers with a peat catchment area, such as the moorland rivers, the spate will be a darker brown; this clears to the colour of whisky. In these waters use a Brown & Gold minnow.

As stated above, water temperature, volume and colour have to be considered, but not only at the start of the day as conditions will alter as the hours pass by. A good practice is to take the air and water temperatures on arrival at the river after breakfast, and to mark the river level with a stick. A March air temperature of 50°F at 10.30 am and water of 42°F are both likely to rise during the day — the water through one or two degrees by 3.00 pm. This rise may trigger a fish to take, particularly if the angler reduces his bait size a fraction if the water level falls at the same time as the temperature rises. Note the starting temperatures I have given for

air and water relative to each other — the former above the latter — if the water is warmer than the air very few fish will be caught in early spring.

Consider the following diary extracts from 1973 on the Taw — this is 15 years ago but the spring runs are still good.

8 March. Beat 3. S Bend. 1.00 pm. 12 lb. 2½ in. Yellow Belly. Water height 2 ft 4 in. Water temp. 43 deg. Air 56°F.
9 March. beat 6. Crockers. 2.00 pm. 13 lb. No. 3 Mepps. Water 2 ft 2 in. 11 March. beats 4 and 5. Dobbs at 12.30 pm. 11 lb. 2¼ in. Yellow Belly. Horestones, at 2.00 pm. 9 lb. Water 2 ft 0 in. Water temp. 43°F. Air 54°F.

The entry of 11 March was concluded with the information

on 10 March the water conditions were similar but there was a cold east wind. I did no good.

Over the four days the water level fell by 4 in. (once down to the 2 ft 3 in. mark after a flood it usually drops an inch a day) enabling a size reduction of ¼ in. in the minnow length. On the clement days the water temperature rose and three of the four fish came after lunch. Nothing was caught on the east wind day when the water would have been cooled both by evaporation at the surface and the coldness of the wind. Look back for a moment at the 9 March entry: the lie in Crocker's Pool is on the far side in quiet water at the slower tail of the pool — hence the use of the Mepps instead of the minnow used elsewhere in faster water. Equally important to choosing the correct size of bait is to ensure that the minnow or

Toby is fished at the correct depth and as slowly as possible — you must scratch the river bed!

One pool may be deeper than the next, and that pool will alter along its length, as will the speed of the current. Such changes, if one is to manoeuvre the bait close to the riverbed at all times, require alteration of the weight at the head of the trace between outside limits of about $\frac{1}{4}-\frac{3}{4}$ oz. This is accomplished by changing the Wye weight or by the addition or removal of clip on 'fold overs'. Screw bombs are rapidly changed without the necessity of removing the swivel head of the bomb — a trio of $\frac{1}{4}$, $\frac{1}{2}$ and $\frac{3}{4}$ oz. bombs would enable you to make any necessary increases or reductions. It is essential that there isn't too much weight or the speed of retrieve would have to be increased to prevent snagging on the bottom; bait must travel slowly in its passage across the river. This slow travel will be assisted if the rod tip is held high, after the bait alights on the water, to keep as much line out of the river as possible — this prevents the current forming a belly in the line and dragging the minnow fast and high across the width of the river. The situation is similar to that already mentioned in mending over a fly-line to achieve the same purpose: a spinning line does not have the weight to be mended over, and the rod is too short, but a high rod tip helps.

The mechanics of deep spinning in the early spring may be rapidly mastered but it takes more than casting ability to catch fish at this time of year — a thorough knowledge of the underwater contours of the pools is necessary. This mental hydrography will only be acquired by returning year after year after year to the same beats, losing

minnows on the bottom and the observation of deep and shallow places in the low water of summer. When this knowledge has been assimilated and stored the angler will be able to cast his bait across the pool, catch it up by a few turns on the reel as it alights and then, with the correct weight in use, allow it to hug the river bed by taking a few turns here, and back winding a turn or two there, to follow the ridges and hollows as the traverse is made.

In support of fishing close to the bottom consider the following diary entry of 18 March 1968 on the Torridge:

Huntingham Beat. Water 44°F. Air 50°F. Height 1 ft 6 in. Coloured. 8$\frac{1}{2}$ lb. Noon. 2 in. metal Yellow Belly.

and again

21 March. Huntingham. Water 1 ft 10 in. 4.30 pm. 14 lb. Lower Boat Pool. 2$\frac{1}{2}$ in. metal Yellow Belly. Fish knocked the minnow and came again to a subsequent cast. I think a metal minnow is better than wood.

These two incidents took place on the Black Horse water managed by Commander Rowe; he only stocked a lightweight wooden Devon with a polythene-tubed centre in the hotel tackle drawer. These wooden Devons were used by the other guests, and they did not readily take fish. One 'plus four'd' inmate spotted the difference and was heard to comment in the hotel bar before I returned from the river on the final day: 'if that chap Bingham has another fish today I'll borrow one of his'.

But wooden minnows have a place when one wishes to fish very deep and extremely slowly employing the system known as the paternoster; this is often

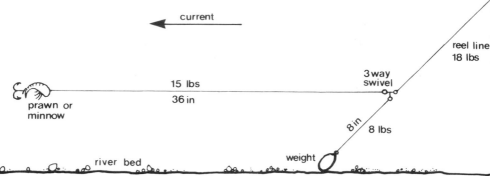

108   *A Peternoster or ledger. To fish a worm, prawn or minnow. The weight, normally of about 1 oz., will rest on the bottom whilst the bait sways in the current. The weak nylon leading to the weight will break before the trace if the outfit snags. The angler is able to 'feel' his way over the river bed as the weight thumps on the bottom. A method suited to fishing an area very slowly.*

used in early season spinning on the Hampshire Avon — renowned for large fish at this time of year. In this method the reel line is attached to one end of a three way swivel and the trace to the other in the normal manner. A length of about 8 in. of thin nylon, perhaps 8 lb test, is tied to the third swivel ring which hangs down; to the end of this short length is tied a pear-shaped weight or screw bomb. This weight establishes contact with the river-bed whilst the wooden minnow swims freely at a slightly higher level. Any snagging will be of the weight; this will be lost on the fine nylon whilst the bait on the trace will be retrieved.

Whilst mentioning the Hampshire Avon I recall 6 March 1975 on Beat 3 at Somerley. I joined my father-in-law for lunch and had about six casts with his rod. The minnow was mounted on a rusty wire trace, which had been used by a friend of his, as had the minnow, for mahseer in India. A salmon of 15 lb took hold and was eventually landed, whereupon it was discovered that the ancient rusty wire had snapped, but in some mysterious way had then become wrapped about one hook of the treble — it was prevented from slipping from the hook solely by the barb.

I have made many references to air and water temperatures: carry a pocket-sized thermometer in a brass case until you are able to tell the temperature by a hand in the river and the touch of the wind on your cheek. The thermometer not only makes possible a decision on the size of bait but will be a guide to those hours when the angler should make his main effort of the day, for he will know when the water has warmed. Take the temperature on arrival at the river, at mid-morning and again at lunch time. If you do not have a thermometer then watch out for insect activity; a hatch of large dark olives as you are eating a sandwich should stimulate you to cease eating and fish at once, for the water has surely warmed. Birds starting to sing is another sign.

When you have become 'tuned in' to the river valley conditions it is possible to recognize those periods when fish take well; don't waste time drinking coffee on the bank, for such clement spells may only last 20 minutes on a cold, hard day. The conditions that trigger a taking period often prevail over several miles of a river at the same time. In addition to the temperature and level factors a shower of rain may do the trick, even if insufficient to alter the flow. My diary records:

26 March 1972. River Taw. Weather had been fine and dry for two weeks, no fish for many days. A little rain last night. 11 am. 8 lb. Top of Stiles Pool. Water height 1 ft 6 in. No. 2 Mepps. At the same time Roger (the policeman) took two fish on Beat 6 in 3 R's and Crockers on a fly, a No. 4 Elverine. Note: Stiles and Beat 6 are roughly 4 miles apart!

Warm water spinning
By the beginning of May it is time to put away the multiplying reel, which is suitable for early spring fishing with heavy baits, and use a fixed spool reel of the Mitchell 300 type already described. If this Mitchell reel is used for early spring fishing the spool should be loaded with nylon of 18 lb test, or thereabouts, but in warm water when smaller lighter baits will be in use it is as well that you reduce the line strength to 15 lb. If a reduction is not made it will be impossible to cast the lighter baits any great distance; a long throw is a necessity in upstream casting.

You now have a choice of two directions in which to cast: down and across as in the cold water method, but not endeavouring to fish so deep, or straight upstream. Before considering down and across in summer consider first whether it is necessary to spin at all: why not fish the fly? With the fly-rod you will be better able to cover the water thoroughly; the fly may be manoeuvred towards and, momentarily, away from your bank; you will have less tackle to carry and the water will be less disturbed by your passing. The fly is more versatile. I do not spin downstream in summer as I am better able to satisfy my requirements in both pleasure and fish for the larder on the fly. I do take the occasional fish on the spinner in autumn fishing downstream, and in summer and autumn on an upstream spoon or Toby.

Back to downstream spinning. It is perfectly possible to cast the small baits required with a short single-handed rod of 7 ft or 7½ ft in length; but the fish have not grown shorter and lighter to match your rod! You may still meet salmon in the 'teens of pounds and above. Use a rod of 8 ft 6 in. or longer — this length provides better control of your minnow and of the hooked fish. I have nothing to write in favour of ultra-short salmon rods.

A favourite bait is the Mepps spoon: the Aglia Regular No. 2 in the gold colour or the Aglia Long No. 1 in copper. Don't forget to cut off the hooks and fit your own as already described. A 1 yd trace of 13 lb nylon will be needed, and at the junction of the two nylons a weight of ¼ oz or ⅜ oz should be attached immediately above a swivel.

A friend paints his small Mepps black, and in the clear low water does very well with them. I once gaffed a salmon of 22 lb for him, which he had enticed to a black Mepps on the Piddle in Dorset; with no added weight he flipped the spoon over to the other side of a small deep pool and let it flutter back to his side using a slow and steady retrieve; just below his bank it was intercepted by this submarine of a fish.

He keeps back from the bank and crouches down; he also dyes his prawns magenta as well as painting the Mepps black. He is a successful fisher because he stalks his fish and uses his head; he waits until the sun is off the water, or has gone behind a tree, or he starts before it has risen; he will fish at once after a thunderstorm or during a gale. I remember him going to Scotland to fish the upstream worm, a method requiring above average skill; he was full of expectation but had no worms to take with him having been let down by the supplier — instead he took some leather bootlaces as a substitute!

The method adopted for the 22 lb fish from the Piddle is the standard procedure for light summer spinning: a small lure, a little weight and a steady retrieve across the river with the lure revolving close to the surface; salmon will rise from the bottom to intercept. The Flopy, the small rubber plug already described, should also be fished down and across, but may be retrieved faster than the Mepps. This plug sets up a vibration as it jiggles back within a foot of the surface. In heavy, much-coloured summer water you may again revert to a Devon minnow or a Toby, but no great weight would be needed, and the metal minnow should be replaced by a plastic Spey as the river depth is not likely to be so great as in spring.

Upstream casting is the only summer spinning I find truly exciting. The slashing turn of a taking fish, close to the surface, in a hurry, seemingly angry, sets the heart pounding. A large bait is better than a small one: a No. 3 or No. 4 Mepps or, best of all, a 3 in., 12 g. Toby in a copper colour. It is essential to know the salmon lies because you must cast upstream some yards beyond the lie. Wait a second or two after the bait alights to allow it to sink a foot; then reel back a trifle faster than the current. It is possible to reel back too fast to be attractive, but there is no need to worry that the speed is too great to be caught — salmon are able to move at a very remarkable pace; frighten one by showing yourself against the sky and it will depart so rapidly that its ability to avoid the rocks on the escape route is truly amazing. One does not always see the upstream take, particularly if the bait is attacked at the full length of the cast as the retrieve commences. When the salmon takes the line just stops, there is then a head shaking, the angler tightens and the fish usually comes down river for a few yards before starting its fight. There is no doubt the fish is very surprised for he almost certainly has not seen the angler and, with the current to help, he may be brought back at once to a close controlled position.

Almost all fish taken when you cast upstream are well-hooked. This is because they have to take at speed, with a wide open mouth, and on the turn to face upstream after the take — in consequence the treble almost always settles into the scissors. The fish does not rise in advance of the arrival of the bait, the sudden appearance of which must be startling, it shoots up from the bottom as the lure goes over its head, chases, engulfs and then turns. Whereupon, the hooks catch up in the corner of the mouth as the line tightens from behind. You may, therefore, play such fish with confidence, provided you give a good hard pull as soon as the fish is felt, for this will drive in the large hooks that otherwise might drop out of the hard and bony mouth.

Typical of summer upstream fishing is the following diary entry:

14 July 1976. Test. Longbridge Pool. 3 pm. U/S [upstream] No. 4 Mepps. 6 lb grilse. Also 5.30 pm. Hospital Pool. U/S No. 4 Mepps. 4 lb sea trout.

and again:

12 June 1977. Test. Rookery. Just above point of Island Pool. No. 5 U/S Mepps. 9 lb with sea lice.

In the case of 12 June the use of a really large upstream bait is justified if the water is high.

7 Natural bait

The prawn

Today, when salmon are less plentiful and anglers are present on the river bank in greater numbers than in the past, one must have every sympathy with the owner or manager of a stretch of salmon water who bans the use of the prawn. We have to live and fish in the present age in close proximity to the next man, whose pleasure we must consider. Over-use of the prawn, day after day, will spoil the fishing of others who will then dislike the angler who is causing the trouble: in consequence, unless he is very thick skinned, he will not enjoy himself either! Moderation is needed; divide your time between fly, spinning and the prawn if all these methods are allowed and appeal to you. How moderation may be enforced is a problem that many have failed to solve, and therefore management that allows the prawn must expect it to be overdone. At times this method catches many fish, particularly in low water, but it does upset the salmon which become scared and almost uncatchable after being tried by many anglers. Catches fall off and do not pick up until a spate brings up new inhabitants to the pools.

I gained more knowledge of salmon behaviour in the four or five years in which I fished the prawn than I gained over many seasons of fishing the fly and artificial spinning baits. Useful knowledge of salmon actions was learnt, but the pleasure in the fishing was not great, and I always felt slightly guilty. I have not fished the prawn for the last ten years.

The most exciting form of prawn fishing is to endeavour to catch a salmon which you can actually see, whilst you do your best to remain out of sight. A fish is most likely to be visible in the clear water of the chalk streams; walk up the river looking into the likely places with polaroid spectacles: a yard off and just to the rear of a groyne; in a gap between weed beds; at the point where the fan-shaped splay of a pool shallows out above the run-off; below the roots of a tree. As suggested, walk up your beat not down, for you will see more; keep back 2 or 3 yd from the bank; be careful that your shadow does not precede you and fall on the water.

It is not surprising that salmon will be found in the same lies if you visit the beat daily, weekly, or irregularly — the places they have chosen suit them. On your investigating walk it is likely that some fish will spot you before you see them - the first you will know of this is the sudden movement as the salmon shoots into cover, or disturbs sand or mud in accelerating: don't despair, he will be back, if not in five minutes then in an hour, or two hours; if he does not return another fish will take his place. Of course you cannot fish spot in the full rivers of early spring — it is a summer occupation in low water and good light. Tackle requirements are very similar to those for spinning, but you must have a long rod of not less than 10 ft if you are not to be disadvantaged when stalking a salmon. A long rod enables the prawn to be placed in front of the salmon whilst the angler remains crouched and hidden behind vegetation on the bank — every extra foot of reach is a help. The fixed spool reel will be needed with the 18 lb monofilament line terminating at a swivel: to the swivel is attached a trace of 15 lb nylon and then the prawn. Weight will be needed at the line/trace swivel, for the prawn must be fished close to the bottom in order to waive about and, if possible, be held in front of the salmon's nose.

Weight may be used in the paternoster, leger style or, as in the Hillman ball-type of weight, just clipped to the swivel. Do not use a trace of less than 15 lb: the favourite safe haven of a hooked salmon in a chalk stream is a weed bed from which he must be drawn by a downstream pull.

Prawns come in different sizes and states of preservation — there is not much to be written in favour of the large, soft, well-matured specimens that may be purchased from the fishmonger's trays. You must do better than that. Such prawns are soft, overcooked, and soon fall to pieces in use — they also rapidly become smelly! Purchase 2–3 lb of fresh prawns straight out of the sea; place these in a saucepan of boiling water until they turn pink; then remove them at once before they become soft. Add a magenta dye to the water if you wish — the colour seems to be an added

attraction. Separate the still-hot prawns on a rough towel and dry with a hair dryer. Package in sixes in small labelled polythene bags — small, medium, large — then freeze, and you will have a supply for a year or two. The large prawns may be used early in the season and the small ones in the summer: choice of size follows the same principles as in the selection of large or small flies or minnows. A prawn preserved in this manner is tough and will stand up to casting for a considerable time; it will also retain all its legs and whiskers — most of these are missing on fishmonger's specimens.

There are many ways of mounting the prawn; the number of devices reflecting the ability of salmon to nip, suck, take in and blow out, and otherwise fiddle with the bait without falling victim to the hooks. The Tony Allen prawn mount enables one treble to be inserted amongst the whiskers at the head of the prawn whilst a second, smaller treble may be moved on a slide of wire to hang down in the legs of the prawn. This mount is particularly useful in hooking those salmon that suck at prawns with eggs — berried prawns as they are called. In attaching the Tony Allen mount the trace nylon should be tied to the bend at the tail of the slide with a tucked half-blood knot; the double slide wires are led up between the legs and the larger treble is hidden in the whiskers at the head into which one of the three hooks is anchored. The whole is then wrapped about with several turns of thin pink electric wire — this may be obtained by unravelling a cable. When the prawn has been mounted the two tail flaps should be broken off: this reduces the appearance of the bait, but if left on they may act

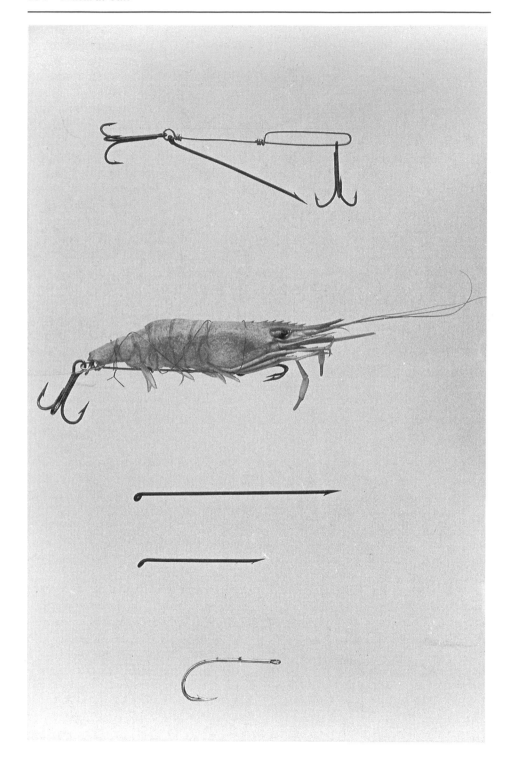

110 *Fishing a salmon pool.*

as a vane in the current, causing the prawn to twist, turn and lie on its side in an unnatural manner. Perhaps the Tony Allen mount is too successful to be acceptable. The last time I fished with prawn was with Tony, its inventor, in 1977 on the Rookery Beat of Broadlands on the Test. The diary records:

109 Top *Tony Allen prawn mount; can be used without the Partridge pin, in which case the double slide would be at the tail of the prawn as described in the text.* Middle *The trace is tied to the ring at the tail of the prawn. Some anglers snap off the spear; tail of prawn has been removed to prevent it acting as a vane in the water flow.* Lower *Partridge T2 prawn and shrimp pins.* Bottom *Sliced worm hook.*

2 Oct. C.R.B. North Bridge.
10.30 am. Prawn. $4\frac{1}{2}$ lb.
2 Oct. C.R.B. Trees Pool. 3.00 pm.
Prawn. 7 lb.
2 Oct. Tony. Ash Tree. 10.00 am.
Prawn. 14 lb.
2 Oct. Tony. North Bridge. 3.30 pm.
Prawn. $7\frac{1}{2}$ lb.

To mount a small prawn thread a $1\frac{1}{2}$ in. Partridge T2 prawn pin on to the trace before knotting on a Partridge X1 treble of size No. 10. Insert the pin into the full length of the body of a straightened prawn starting under the tail. Pierce the head with one hook of the treble; the trace will lie outside the body hidden between the legs and the whole may be held in position with turns of the red wire.

Some anglers snap off the spear of the prawn because they fear that this spike may disuade salmon from taking hold of the head and thus, in a single treble mount, avoid being hooked. I remove the spear, for a salmon often takes his time before accepting a prawn and, with excellent sight, no doubt gives the bait a very close inspection. That salmon are able to grip a prawn across the body, avoiding the hook at the head, has been demonstrated many times — I have even known them detach a prawn from the mount and slide it up the trace. The delicacy and accuracy of a salmon's snout is almost beyond belief.

Two days ago (mid-October 1986) I was observing salmon from a distance of 10 or 12 ft whilst photographing them through a polarized filter as they swirled about and played close to the bed of the river. One pair were particularly loving — the cock fish approached the hen at right angles and nuzzled her down the length of her body from the nose to the tail, not once, but several times. The hen became agitated as his snout approached her tail and when he did this once too often they both drifted away. It was almost as though he was sniffing his mate, and this confirmed in my mind the desirability of rubbing one's hands in soil, mud or on grass before mounting a prawn — human hands smell!

When equipped an angler has to decide whether to attempt to catch a fish he can see, or just fish the river. Let us first consider the visible victim. Our intention is to place the prawn about 6 in. or a foot in front of the salmon's nose and then hold it there. An advance assessment must be made of the depth of the river and the speed of the current in order that a correct weight is attached. This done the bait is cast out above and beyond the fish in order that, in sinking, it is swept around to the desired position. The reaction of a sal-

mon may be watched and will vary: he may dash away; he may do nothing unless the prawn actually touches him, when he will probably swim off or swing a little to one side; or he may take at once. There are other possibilities: he may take and blow out before you can strike; he may take after the prawn has been suspended in front of him for half an hour; or he may move forward and pick up a prawn that has been allowed to rest on the bottom.

If the salmon's mouth is seen to open, and this is readily observed, particularly from upstream, strike at once or you may be too late, for a salmon is able to eject a prawn with great rapidity. Care must be taken not to allow the prawn to swim into the blind area behind salmon — they at once become restless and usually swim away; if this happens the fish will often return to the same lie within a few minutes. The ledger system is the best way of holding a prawn in front of a salmon because the weight may be allowed to act as an anchor on the river bed whilst the prawn swings freely in the current.

The prawn may also be used to fish the river when the angler does not have knowledge of the exact whereabouts of a fish. Cast out and let the bait swing around downstream in the same manner as fishing a deep minnow, but as slowly as possible. Because the angler cannot see when a salmon has mouthed the prawn he has to rely on touch. Sensitive vibrations of a fish nipping at the bait will be achieved by holding the nylon line between the fingers of the left hand. Any activity at the other end should prompt an immediate strike; this may not be successful — salmon are adept at nipping a prawn without becoming hooked.

Sometimes the tremors reaching your fingers will be the work of eels. In fact in summer on the Test, whilst having lunch, we fished for eels with half a prawn as bait on a single hook: this was left resting on the bottom until a twitching of the line alerted us to the presence of something; it was always an eel and never a salmon!

To ensure that the prawn is fishing close to the river bed use the method known as sink-and-draw. In this the rod is raised a foot or two to lift the weight from the bottom; it is then lowered sharply — the slight tap when the weight makes contact with the river bed will be transmitted up the line. Sink-and-draw is particularly suitable for fishing the deep fast narrow necks of pools; this may require the use of more than an ounce of lead to hold the bait against the pressure of the current. With a long rod in these places it is often not necessary to cast with the reel bail arm open, sufficient line may be raised by the length of the rod and a yard or two drawn in by hand to be released with each cast, to obviate the use of the reel handle.

The prawn may also be spun, in which case it is necessary to purchase a mount with clear plastic vanes at the end of a single metal pin. I have not used this device because an unnatural movement is induced in the bait — as a boy I never saw a prawn spin in and out of the beds of seaweed whilst going after them with a net. Despite my dislike of spinning prawns it must be acknowledged that the spun-prawn takes salmon. More natural, exciting and satisfying is to drift the prawn below a cork float. A pike float is suitable and readily adjustable up and down the line on the central wooden pin; the wine cork from your lunch bottle may be used if encircled with a couple of elastic bands under which is passed the reel line. The prawn is mounted in the usual manner with a trace of one yard, at the head of which should be a swivel and then a small lead. The float should be adjusted on the line above the weight to a position which will allow the prawn to drift downstream a foot or so above the river bed. This method is exciting: the bobbing float reminding me of my earliest float fishing days for roach and perch on the Shropshire lake at the age of 8 or 9.

The shrimp

Shrimps may be purchased and preserved in the same manner as prawns for fishing a tough, whiskered and well-legged specimen. Frozen in half-dozens a pack may be removed from the freezer, broken open and the six specimens placed between damp pads of foam in a flat tobacco tin. Carried in the pocket in this manner the shrimps will not be broken in transit along the river bank — a shrimp readily breaks in half, being more delicate than a prawn. Spare packs of shrimps, when taken from the deep freezer, should be placed in a wide-mouthed Thermos flask packed with ice. This reserve may be left in the car or in the fishing hut adjacent to the river.

Shrimps may be mounted on a long-shanked single hook, the eye of the hook being pushed into the head and half way up the body, which is kept straight by an inserted piece of fine wire such as a straightened paper clip. The single hook, however, may twist in the body; the weight of the hook then tends to make the shrimp swim on its side. The best method is to thread a short Partridge eyed shrimp pin onto the trace and insert this pin back into the length of the body from below the tail; a small treble, No. 10 is about right, is then placed in the whiskers, with the nylon laid between the legs; the whole is then wrapped sparingly with fine copper wire.

If the shrimp is to be fished off a fly rod one cannot cast a 1 yd trace with a weight and swivel; instead a little fine lead wire may be wrapped about the pin before it is inserted and plain nylon used as a leader. It is as well to prepare weighted pins in advance. Take a $1\frac{1}{2}$ in. pin, place the barbed end in a fly vice and wrap 0.37 mm lead wire in side by side turns around the shank for two-thirds of the length, terminating at the eye.

The shrimp is a killing bait for low clear water; more so than the prawn. It may be fished off the spinning rod and fixed spool reel in the manner already described for prawn, but in general less weight is required in the low water conditions. The shrimp is suitable for gentle casting off a fly-rod, but this is only possible in small to medium rivers. A long cast applies too much strain on the shrimp which will break up. In the smaller rivers a shrimp, weighted as described with a leaded pin, fishes well when drifted across a pool downstream of the angler. I recall fishing in this way one summer day on the Beat known as Lee Park on the Test. The weather was hot, sunny and no doubt I was in my shirt sleeves and had discarded the net. Fishing was tiring, my feet were hot in gum-boots and my back ached from casting the shrimp on a long split-cane fly-rod. The bait dollied about out of sight below the surface in a gently flowing run between the banks of weed which

spread out from each bank. Without any pressure or pull a grilse took the shrimp — very gently. Almost with an apology for withdrawing it from my keeping, the grilse terminated the drifting movement of the shrimp, just as softly as one would pick up a dandelion seed head without disturbing the fluff. When we set about each other he was eventually persuaded to beach himself on a mud bank where the hook fell out before I could take a hold of his slimness; he jumped back into the river, leaped with joy — but back onto the mud bank. He was the most unlucky fellow.

The worm

If you were sent on a personal survival course in summer without any food, but placed by a salmon river with a variety of rods, reels, lines and hooks a sensible course would be to set about finding a couple of large lob worms. With these you could secure a baked salmon supper, always supposing that a box of matches was to hand to light a fire. If a week had to be spent on the river no doubt a diet of fish would become monotonous, but some variety would be experienced in eating sea trout and wild brownies, for all will take a worm— in fact it is no easy matter to discourage the brown trout from stealing from the salmon!

The last time I fished the worm with persistence was in 1972. In that summer and in the previous season four salmon fell to my rod by this method in Scotland on the Isle of Mull where I was on a family holiday; two more were caught in the same manner by Bill, my father-in-law. It was an experience of great interest, excitement and satisfaction — skill was needed for we only had fly-rods. Our excuse was that our wives wanted salmon for dinner in the evening in the farmhouse. I say 'excuse' for worming is considered not 'the done thing' by many — perhaps they have not fished the worm and are without experience of the difficulties, not only in the fishing but in the hard work to be done to obtain the bait. To fish the worm habitually is not the wish of most salmon anglers, the fly is more pleasurable, but it is an effective method and many see little wrong with using a worm if one really needs a salmon for the table. It can be an emergency solution.

The Mull successes came about in the following manner. We had taken the house known as Ardura for a fortnight in 1971, together with the mile and a half of the right bank of the Lussa which goes with the estate. This small spate river has a run of grilse, small summer salmon and sea trout which enter the river in numbers from the beginning of July. We fished the fly for the first week in low clear water. Fish were there all right, we could see them in the river and jumping in the estuary where they were pursued by filmy-eyed seals that surfaced close to our boat when we spun for mackerel. Some solution had to be found. The house had a fishing record book in which the entry of the tenant who had left before our arrival intrigued me 'we might have had success if a bit more skilled with the worm' — there it was, in black and white; others did it, why not us? Worms came from the vegetable garden; Bill, who has principles, called them garden rangers and that didn't sound so bad. We mounted the rangers on salmon fly hooks from which we stripped the dressing — this was a chance to be rid of patterns

that one carried but never trusted.

A little lead was needed   thin strips were cut from an old pipe with a pocket knife. The outfit on which Bill took the first fish was a 9 ft split-cane trout rod, a No. 6 floating fly line, a strong untapered leader with a tiny piece of lead crimped on, and the worm on the fly hook. Probably there were two worms; Bill has some experience in the matter, although he does not readily admit the skill acquired in his youth, and he always insists in covering the hook point. The diary reads:

6. 7. 8 August 1971. R. Lussa. Mull. Bill took a salmon of $5\frac{3}{4}$ lb on a worm in Sea Pool. Next day I had one of 7 lb and on a Sunday (!). On 8th I had one of 6 lb in Pedlar's. Took the Pedlar's fish as the water rose at the start of a small spate. Several small sea trout to $1\frac{1}{4}$ lb also taken.

The spate came down very coloured. It was impossible to see into the river and, because there was no doubt the salmon couldn't see out, I took up position on the right bank of Pedlar's and cast out the worm with a swinging motion on a 12 ft split-cane fly-rod. There was no weight on the leader. The worms flew over to the far side and dropped under the high bluff opposite where they were at once taken by a salmon. There was no waiting, trembling of lines, tugs, touches or little pulls - he just took with vigour, and that was that. But the midges were terrible and just as hungry as the salmon.

The following year we returned with the fly-rods but I also fitted a single-handed split-cane with a fixed-spool reel and 18 lb monofilament. The result was as follows:

1972. R. Lussa. Took three salmon of 5 lb, 6¼ lb and 6¾ lb. Had two good spates during the two weeks from 5–18 August. Torosay (left bank) took five salmon from their side of the river during the first spate which coincided with Spring tides, and nothing on the second spate that came at Neaps. We also had a number of finnock and four sea trout of between 1 and 1½ lb. Torosay keeper told me they catch salmon on the worm and ⅜ oz Toby.

Looking back on these experiences it is clear we improvized with success—and great fun it was too. At the same time it would have been more productive, if not more enjoyable, to have gone prepared.

Take the worm first. They may be purchased, but one can dig them up or collect them at night from the lawn. They may be stored in a polythene box, filled with damp moss, and should be kept in a cool outhouse. In need, a worm will almost always be found at the riverside by turning over large stones. As to the hook, many complicated multiple arrangements are available, but a single hook of good size, No. 1 or No. 2 is satisfactory. If the hook has two 'slices' on the shank these up-pointing barbs will keep part of the worm above the bend. A whipped-on short bristle will serve the same purpose. With a good-sized lob worm one can work the body up the shank until the eye of the hook and the nylon knot are enclosed in the body; a second worm will then cover the barb and the point. Many anglers ensure that the point of the hook is buried out of sight inside the body; others leave the point proud in order that it may more readily take hold in the mouth of the fish. Both methods work; in any event the point almost always becomes exposed after a few minutes fishing.

Consider fishing methods. One may cast upstream or downstream; use a fly-rod or spinning equipment. Take upstream fishing first. A single-handed fly-rod may be used with a floating fly line and a leader of 15 lb test, or the fixed spool and monofilament. If the rod has a butt extension this will relieve your wrist when a salmon is being played. I have, at times, used a double-handed 12 ft fly-rod, but it is easier to control the line to be shot through the rod rings if two hands are not required in the casting and the left hand is free. Fast false casts to work out distance cannot be made with the fly-line or the worm will fly off the hook, but it is possible to draw as much line off the reel as one requires before starting and, with one or two swings, shoot the whole over and out across the river in a diagonal upstream direction. In this case the worm will drift down and swing in to the angler's side.

A little weight in the form of a split shot will add depth without the outfit being likely to catch on the bottom; too much weight on an upstream cast almost always results in snagging. The floating fly-line gives good control and may be retrieved over the right forefinger with the left hand. If the worm stops one should feel for any movement at the other end; if there is a tug or twitch give the salmon time to engulf the bait by waiting at least half a minute before raising the rod. Occasionally a salmon takes with vigour, moves away and hooks himself. Worming with the fly-rod is best confined to shallow water in summer, for the method of upstream casting does not allow the use of much, if any, weight.

In heavier water it is as well to use a long spinning rod and a fixed-spool reel, the spool filled with 18 lb nylon and the trace being of 15 lb breaking strain. As the main risk of using too much weight is of the lead becoming jammed in a snag or between rocks it is sensible to use a leger system: the weight being attached by fine nylon of 8 lb which will break first, allowing the worm and line to swing free. Cast over to the middle of the river and fish the near side. The rod should be held high to keep as much line out of the water as possible — this will reduce the risk of snagging. The length of cast may then be extended. The intention is to feel the lead bump the river bed from time to time as the worm swings to the angler's side. The fishing must be slow; any hesitation or pause in the bait's progress should cause the angler to take the line between the fingers of his left hand to detect twitching by a fish. If movement is felt do not strike until at least half a minute has passed — if an immediate strike is made the bunch of worms will almost certainly be plucked out of the mouth of the fish.

I remember climbing a tree to drop a bunch of worms in front of a salmon that I could see, and which ultimately pulled the scales down to 9 lb. The worms plopped into the river 3 or 4 yd upstream of the fish; as they sank he rose to meet them, opened his mouth, shut it and I struck. Result? the bunch of worms was blown out into the pool. I wound them up to my perch, made a repair, added a fresh specimen and tried again. The fish rose, the white-edged mouth opened for the second time, in went the worms, the lips closed and I did nothing. The salmon returned to its lie with a smug expression. Up my tree I waited, cramped, stiff and trembling. And waited. And struck. All was well.

It is fortunate that the least suitable conditions for the fly may be the best for the worm. In consequence, many an unsuccessful holiday has been saved on the final day by the production of a tin of worms from the gillie's pocket. Bill fished the fly with patience on the Snizort on Skye for several days without success in rather thick October water — on the last day he took a salmon off the fly rod with the gillie's worm. In my view such use of this bait is acceptable. It does seem that the worm fishes best in warm water, over 55°F, than when the river is cold. A spate is really the peak worming time, not a heavy flood, just a rise, usually rather dirty, but sufficient to activate the salmon from torpor after a period of drought. Such water conditions are not good for the fly, owing to poor visibility, but a worm will be found and taken, perhaps by smell. If smell is a helpful factor then, as with the shrimp and prawn, be sure to rub your hands in mud or earth before handling the bait.

8 Odds and ends

Clothing and waders

The clothing a fisherman needs will vary with the time of year; consider the requirements for a cold spring. Four thin layers of clothes are warmer than two which are thick; wool is more comfortable than man-made fibres and tends to 'breathe' better. A good choice would be a wool shirt, vest and sweater; Long John's, if wading, will help to keep the legs warm, and there should be room inside the waders for two pairs of socks. Whether one intends to wade or not in March thigh waders will keep in the heat and keep out the rain.

A waxed jacket is a good outer garment but must be long enough to overlap the top of the thigh waders: many jackets are too short and efficiently channel the rain into the tops of the wearer's boots! Always take your waders with you when purchasing a fishing coat and see that the hem comes down far enough. The coat should have a detachable hood of good depth to enclose your cap as well as your head. If you do not like wearing a hood because it reduces your hearing, and I like to be able to hear a salmon splash, then a deerstalker and towelling scarf will keep the rain from trickling down your neck. There should be at least four good-sized pockets in which to place tackle: these will make it unnecessary to carry a fishing bag, which is a nuisance when casting. The coat should be equipped with a large poacher's pocket that will accept a 10 lb salmon when tied nose to tail — if a plastic bin liner is kept folded in this pocket the salmon may be placed in the liner to keep the coat clean. Mittens are a must in the cold weather.

Thigh waders are usually sold with a strap for attachment to the belt that holds up the angler's trousers. This is an uncomfortable arrangement which may cause anxiety! A better system is to attach a short strap or cord to the buckle at the top hem of the wader and fit a split ring at the top end of the cord; take a cloth strap of adjustable length; fit clips at each end, pass over the neck under the coat and clip to the wader split rings. As to the waders: you can have a strong studded pair, which will be heavy; or a lighter pair with a cleated sole. I have not found studded soles grip better than cleated.

For summer fishing where much walking is involved, thigh waders are very sticky to wear, particularly in strong sunlight. My practice has been to purchase an additional pair of the light thigh waders and cut them off at knee level. Such an arrangement provides a gum boot 6 in. taller than a wellington boot and costs about the same.

Waders should be hung up in the dark when not in use. Black rubber lasts longer than green, being less readily perished in daylight. I have never owned a pair of chest waders, although I have borrowed a pair from time to time. It is as well to remember that the deeper you wade the more chance there is of being swept off your feet, particularly if not using a wading staff and you do not know the river like the back of your hand. I would not invest in chest waders unless I lived by a river where they were a necessity.

For summer fishing it is most comfortable to wear a sweater and a fishing waistcoat, which leaves the arms free and keeps them cool. The waistcoat is a splendid garment for it has many pockets, with a particularly large one at the back in which a light raincoat may be carried. A number of makes are available with a larger back pocket which will hold a raincoat or a salmon, or both. The problem of summer fishing is perspiration. If the angler prefers a coat to a waistcoat then he would be well advised to consider the Wychwood range of jackets manufactured by Gore-Tex. This fabric is waterproof but also 'breathes', allowing perspiration to escape. A light jacket in their range is the Warwick. These coats are obtainable from Farlows of Pall Mall, London, and from William Powell & Son of Birmingham.

Other equipment and snippets

Polaroid spectacles
It is best to have a filter which lets through as much polarized light as possible - quite the opposite to a pair of conventional dark glasses. An excellent example is sold under the name Multisport. They have lenses of various colours: grey, tan and yellow (I can recommend the grey ones), and a case is supplied with two sets of side arms — straight and curved. Both arms are adjustable for length. The flexible arms curve behind the ears and do not fall off when one leans forward. The spectacles are manufactured by Multisport Optical, 9 Ham Lane, Powick, Worcester, WR2 4RA.

Fly boxes
The aluminium fly box with clips is not for treble-hooked tube flies or Waddingtons. Hardy's market the Neroda salmon fly box which will hold single, double and treble hooked flies on foam pads. The same firm has a zipped leather fly wallet which is particularly suitable for tube flies and Waddingtons. The best box I know for tube flies is free. It is the container for two one hundred metre spools of Platil Strong. The box has two additional plastic dividers packed alongside the nylon: when fitted into the slots provided they make a six compartment box. Place the flies in the bottom of each section and hold them from rattling in the pocket with six pieces of foam cut from a cheap car sponge.

Tackle check list
Whether fishing the fly or spinning in spring or summer the following are common to both and must be taken to the river:
Rod
Gye net
Priest on a string to loop over neck
Scissors on a string to loop over neck
Polaroid spectacles
Waders or boots

Fishing coat, or waistcoat with folding
  waterproof
Rod licence (England and Wales)
Cord to carry a salmon
Midge cream (summer)
Mittens (cold weather)
Bag of spare clothes in car

In addition you need for the fly:
Reel plus floating line (summer)
Reel spool plus sink tip line (summer)
Reel plus fast sinking line (cold water)
Spool 15 lb Platil Strong for leaders
Flies in box
and/or for spinning:
Fixed spool reel 18 lb line or
Multiplier reel 18 lb line (heavy spin-
  ning only)
Fixed spool reel or spare spool 15 lb
  line (summer)
15 lb nylon for trace (heavy spinning)
13 lb nylon for trace (summer)
Box of baits
Tin of weights
Oil can for reel

Carrying salmon
The easiest way to carry a salmon is to
loop a length of cord over the tail, settle
it around the wrist behind the adipose
fin, pass through the mouth and out of
the gills, then tie the ends together as in
the black and white illustration. To
carry a fish with the fingers through the
gills on one side and the tail dragging
on the ground is neither comfortable for
the angler, whose arm will be bent at
the elbow, nor good for the salmon's
appearance; additionally the gill will
break open in time.

Single-bank fishing
The question is often raised whether an
angler fishing a single-bank beat may
cast over to the far bank in a river which

may be fully covered from both sides.
My view is that you may do so with
the following consideration paid to the
angler on the far side: on arrival at a
pool being fished from the opposite
bank wait until the occupant has ceased,
and only then follow him down. On no
account start in front of him. In this
way neither will cast under the feet of
the other. It is also incumbent on your
opposite number to move on steadily
down the pool and then on down the
river, and not to fish back up for a
second go at the best places. He could,
of course, start in behind and follow you
down if he wished to cover the water
for a second time.

Do not wade out more than one third
of the width of the river.

If the angler on one bank is fishing
the fly and the man on the other side is
spinning or fishing a natural bait such
as worm or prawn, it would be courte-
ous to allow the fly man to cover the
water first, for he is likely to cause less
disturbance.

Freezing salmon
There are various opinions on whether a
salmon should be frozen whole without
being cleaned, cleaned and then frozen
whole, or cleaned, cut up into pieces
and frozen. My own practice is to clean
all fish as soon as possible after leaving
the river. Grilse of 4, 5 and 6 lb are then
frozen whole after cleaning and cutting
out the gill rakes: they are placed in
individual polythene bin liners and
labelled with date, weight, the name
of the river, and any comments on
condition. Larger fish have the head and
tail removed after cleaning and are then
cut into pieces of 2 and 3 lb as required,
each section being placed in an individual polythene bag with a weight

111 *A piece of baler twine used to carry a salmon.*

112 *Fish carried in this manner will not scrape on rocks or the ground.*

113 *Fish are weighed on return from the river.*

label. There are usually three pieces from each fish; these are all put into a plastic shopping holder, labelled with date, river and condition and then frozen. Do not freeze large fish whole, unless you have a party in mind which requires that weight of salmon, for you then have to thaw out the complete salmon, which may be above immediate requirements, or cut a piece off with a hacksaw - a difficult task!

Time of day to fish

In February and March - the second half of the day

April - the middle of the day until about 6 pm, or when it becomes cold

May - the whole day

June to September - early morning and late evening

October - the middle of the day

The above are the best times, but fish all the hours available if the water is in good order, even if other factors, such as relative air/water temperatures, are not encouraging. You never know! There is a saying 'it is the man who moves his feet who catches the salmon' in other words keep at it and keep moving up and down your beat.

Rod licences

In England and Wales, but not (yet?) Scotland, a rod licence is needed to fish with rod and line. The licences are available in these categories:

● Freshwater fish and eels (other than trout, migratory trout and salmon);
● Trout, freshwater fish and eels (but excluding migratory trout and salmon);
● Salmon (including trout, migratory trout, freshwater fish and eels).

Licences may be purchased as valid for one day, one week, or the season; they are valid only in the area of the issuing water authority. If one buys a licence in the area of South West Water it is not valid in the area of Thames Water and so on. The rod licence does not entitle the angler to fish in any water without the permission of the owner of that water, who himself must have a licence to fish in his own river or lake. In some cases the management of a river may

114 *They are then cleaned and washed.*

pay a bulk contribution to the water authority to cover all visiting anglers; in this case the angler does not need an individual licence.

The fisheries and recreation departments of the water authorities generally issue an angling guide of their area. These booklets are inexpensive, full of information on available fisheries, close seasons, licence distributors and so on.

Tying a Black Dart tube fly

The dressing has been given earlier: here is a detailed list of the materials required and the sequence of dressing.

Materials:
Vice, preferably with rotary jaws
Darning needle on which to mount the tube

Dubbing needle
Pair of fine scissors
Spigot bobbin holder for the Naples silk
Whip finish tool - voluntary - fingers are better
B type socketed polythene tube
Black Naples silk
Black floss silk
Fine lead wire of 0.37 mm
Oval gold tinsel No. 16
Clear varnish
Black varnish
Buck tail — orange
Jungle cock — two feathers

The sequence for tying a $1\frac{1}{4}$ in. tube is as follows:

1 Place pointed end of needle in vice, the tube is then slid in a tight fit onto the needle with the socket at the vice end.

2 Naples silk is run in side by side turns from the head of the tube to within $\frac{1}{10}$ in. of the end of the socket where

the gold tinsel is tied in and taken in eight turns up towards the head, and tied down, but not cut off.

3 Tie in black floss, and then fractionally towards the head the lead wire which is wound first in side by side turns to within $\frac{1}{5}$ in. of the tube head, where it is tied down and cut off. The floss silk follows on top of the lead and is tied down at the head and cut off.

4 The gold tinsel is picked up and wound in three or four ribbing turns, in a spiral, stopped short of the end of the tube by $\frac{3}{10}$ in., tied down and cut off.

5 The tube is then rotated on the needle as sparse tufts of bucktail are laid on at the head — each tuft being glued in with a small spot of the clear varnish. The bucktail surrounds the head, and is trimmed off just behind the flange at the front of the tube. The length of the bucktail should exceed the hook by about $\frac{1}{2}$ in.

6 Tie in one jungle cock feather on each side; the feather is to reach almost to the gold tinsel tag. Whip off and paint head with black varnish.

Detailed instructions on dressing tube flies are contained in John Veniards book; *Fly Dressers' Guide*.

The gillie

If you have booked a salmon fishing holiday on a strange river it can make all the difference to have a guide who knows the water; the alternative is to spend a great deal of time finding the pools and lies for oneself, and even the way to the river. Since lies seasonally alter with water height and, with winter floods, the task is never-ending. The gillie himself is constantly adding to his own knowledge, even after many seasons on a length of river. The cost of travel, hotel accounts, tackle, beat rental are considerable on a salmon holiday: the cost of a gillie for two or three days is a small proportion of the whole and may make the difference between success and failure.

If I were employed to gillie I would look upon imparting knowledge of the river as my prime responsibility, coupled with the safety of the person by whom I was employed. It is not the job of the gillie to teach his employer to fish unless requested to do so. The angler should make up his own tackle, attach his leader, tie on his fly — he then has himself to blame if they come undone. I remember hooking and losing a salmon on the fly on the Helmsdale when the fly-knot slipped; it had been tied on by the gillie — his fault maybe, but if I had done the knot myself there could not possibly have been any embarassment. The gillie should be expected to give advice on flies and baits, and the angler would be sensible to accept the advice, at any rate for a while. If the flies suggested do not bring success, the angler may then use his own patterns; he will have confidence in them, but even so the gillie's experience on size should not be lightly disregarded.

It is usually looked upon as the gillie's duty to net or tail an angler's fish. I have managed to do this without loss so far in ten years of running salmon courses, but if I am gillying for someone, as opposed to teaching them, I would make certain that 'the rod' wished me to assist at the netting. If skilled it is safer for a fisherman to net his own salmon provided he can close with the fish, he knows exactly what he is doing and is able to co-ordinate the actions of rod and net. If two people are involved there is the possibility of misunderstanding at the final moment unless they know each other well.

I always net my own salmon if I am able to get to the fish. An obvious exception is when the rod is high above the water and the net must be used at river level. It would be wise for the gillie to ascertain the wishes of his rod in advance. I have twice been involved in the near loss of a salmon whilst teaching: in one case the fish weighed 19 lb and in the other 5 lb. In both cases lack of co-ordination was involved owing to the rod being immediately behind the netsman, myself, and unable to see that the salmon had entered the bag of the net, the angler continued to apply pressure and drew the salmon out. Fortunately, both instances ended happily.

Knots

A single turn, wind knot, half Granny, call it what you will, reduces the strength of nylon by 50 per cent. The following knots have a strength of at least 80 per cent of the test rating of the nylon. The list is not exhaustive but will cover all usual requirements. Rapid tying of a knot is the result of learning where to place one's fingers; this comes from following a diagram with thick nylon and then much practice. A knot is tightened readily if the nylon is moistened in the mouth after the turns have been made but before the knot is drawn up.

Tucked Half Blood

This should be used for attaching the treble hook that is to be drawn into the socket at the tail of a tube fly — also for swivels, weights, prawn mounts, eyed worm hooks and spinning baits. It is a

115 *Glance up the leader regularly: a wind knot will show against the sky.*

simple knot to tie and has a great many uses, including the attachment of both monofilament and braided backing to the empty reel spool. Take two turns of the backing around the spool. Then, with the free end, tie the tucked half blood against the backing itself, tighten and slide down to the spool.

The Turle Knot and Two Circle Turle

The turle is the knot I use for all eyed sea Trout and salmon flies, with the exception of a large eyed salmon fly of size No. 2 and above, in which case the two circle Turle will ensure that the knot does not pull through the eye of the fly. Avoid flies which do not have room behind the eye for the one or two coils of nylon to settle in front of the dressing. Both Turle knots ensure that the fly stays in line with the leader which passes straight into the eye of the fly. The tucked half blood is not suitable for eyed flies as it may slip around the circumference of the eye and pull from the side.

Sheet Bend

When fishing with a fly-rod of 12 ft or above join the leader of 9 ft, or less, to the fly line with a sheet bend. This knot is clearly visible on the water where it acts as a guide to the position of the fly and, through movement, may indicate when a salmon takes. With the rod substantially longer than the leader there is no risk, when landing a fish, of winding the knot through the point ring of the rod.

Needle or Nail Knot

This has two uses. The first is to attach a short length, or collar, of 1 ft of 20 lb nylon, to the business end of the fly-line. This collar may be tied with a blood knot to the butt of the leader from which the loop has been removed. This enables the line, and then part of the leader, to run in and out of the point ring of a short single-handed fly-rod when you are netting a fish; such an attachment of the leader should always be used in night fishing for sea trout when you cannot see the line/leader junction knot.

An additional advantage of this stream-lined arrangement is that the fly will not catch up on a bulky knot when false casting. The second use is to join the back end of the fly-line to the mon-ofilament backing on the reel. The knot will run freely out through the rod rings when a fish is taking out a length of line greater than the 30 yd of the fly-line. It is not necessary to heat the needle in order to execute this knot, but the darning needle must be of the correct diameter to match the thickness of the nylon.

The Albright Knot

This is used to join braided backing to the fly-line.

The Blood Knot

For joining together lengths of nylon of the same, or not too dissimilar, diam-eters; 20 lb may be joined to 15 lb; 10 lb to 5 lb. But you will find 20 lb to 10 lb would be too great a disparity in diameters, and the knot would slip. This knot is useful in making up tapered leaders. It may also be used to attach a dropper or bob fly: leave 4 or 5 in. of one end of nylon, which would otherwise be trimmed off when the knot has been tyed. The end to be left should be that from up, and not down, the leader—thus, if the knot slips, the fish will still be on the top section of the cast.

Blood Bight Loop

For a loop at the butt end of a leader.

Choice of rivers

The best guide on the market today is *Where to Fish* edited by D. A. Orton, published by Harmsworth. The book covers both coarse and game waters in the British Isles and gives the areas and addresses of the water authorities of England and Wales. Also listed are fishery agents in England, Wales and Scotland and these include many of the major firms of land and estate agents. Information is given on close seasons and rod licence distributors in the regions. Many foreign countries are included and helpful addresses given both at home and abroad. A fishing map of Great Britain and Ireland is at the back of the book.

Another useful publication is *The Salmon Rivers of Scotland* by Derek Mills and Neil Graesser, published by Cassell. This book makes a comprehensive description of the rivers with many maps, some in such detail that the names of pools are noted by the side of each beat. The magazine *Trout & Salmon* of Bretton Court, Peterborough, publishes guides from time to time on available sea trout and salmon fishing, and a useful booklet is their pocket guide to Scottish fishing hotels.

The journal of the Salmon and Trout Association of Fishmonger's Hall, London EC4R 9EL *The Salmon and Trout Magazine* is a mine of information in advertisements to those seeking game waters. The journal is free to members, and those who are concerned with the continued quality and freedom of their sport may consider it advisable to join.

Boat fishing

One of the first salmon I lost was from a boat. This event took place in the early 1950s just below Pontoon Bridge where Lough Conn runs into Lough Cullen in Co. Mayo in the West of Ireland. The bait was a $1\frac{1}{4}$ in. Blue & Silver metal Devon minnow, tied to a 10 lb trace; the rod was short, stiff and of steel. In fact it was an old Slapton pike spinning rod from which I had removed the top foot as a boy in the mistaken belief that a salmon would make short work of a pike rod. I can see it now: the grey shadow rose unexpectedly from the depths as the minnow came into view in the clear water, a great mouth opened and closed, the shadow curved away and I, in shock, raised the stiff rod sharply and 'ping' the thin trace snapped. So much for fishing fine nylon off a stiff rod — one learns!

In boat fishing one of the first requirements is to be comfortable and keep a dry bottom: wear waterproof trousers when it rains and sit on a cushion at all times. I have not done much boat fishing specifically for salmon; my ventures afloat being concerned with sea trout — this will be covered later in this book. As both salmon and sea trout are found in the lochs of Scotland together, and sea trout in greater numbers, one is more likely to be fishing for sea trout and occasionally find oneself with a salmon. This happened to me twice at Scourie in Sutherland in the very early days. We will therefore cover boat fishing for the two fish together in a later chapter.

9 The chub fly and the salmon: a salmon story

The grey and portly chub knew by now almost all those things which were important for his survival in a deep, slow-running stream. He knew the best spot to be by the water entrance to his pool through which food morsels came to sustain his aldermanic three pound bulk, and he occupied that place. He knew the safest hole in the pool and went there rather ponderously when danger threatened, gently displacing by his bulk any small chub in residence. He made no mistakes, took no risks, tolerated no userpers and in a contented restful sort of way just grew steadily larger.

A pollarded willow tree grew on the bank of the pool. It was an old tree whose roots on one side were washed by the stream which undercut the bank, and in these roots the fishes of the stream took refuge in times of danger. A boy of 12 or 13 years sat hidden in the knobbly crown of the tree one day in June. Well-shielded by the leaves he made his preparations. From his pocket he took a tin on which he had written 'chub flies' — he knew they were chub flies as the packet he had purchased in the shop said so. The flies were black and rather too bushy and were the only flies he possessed. In fact they were the only thing he had at the moment to fish with, having left school in a hurry for the river. The boy would have preferred a bumble bee or grasshopper impaled upon a hook but had not had time to catch one after his lessons. He tied the fly to the leader on his rod which was camouflaged by the branches. Peering down into the pool he watched in fascination as the alderman engulfed a green and squirming caterpillar which had slowly descended onto the water at the end of a silken thread. 'Crikey, if only I could get him. Good job I've got my best leader on the rod', he thought as he gently pushed the tip out through the leaves.

The alderman had enjoyed the caterpillar. The skin enclosed more meat and juice than spindly flies, which he found unsatisfactory, being mostly wings and legs. Give him a plump worm or caterpillar any day. He looked up hopefully, cocked his head a little to one side, and was surprised to see a further meal descending on another silken thread. The meal looked like a fat black spider and the chub watched it greedily but without much hope; spiders could go up as well as down, he knew, but he moved a little closer — just in case. The boy's heart thundered as the fish lifted in the water and he dropped the fly with a plop on the placid surface of the stream. There was a bulging swirl, thick white lips engulfed the fly, the line tore off the reel as the alderman realised his mistake and made for the safe place.

The boy slid down the tree, barking knees and forearms, and rushing into the tail of the pool, drew the chub away from the refuge. The battle was short, sharp and final.

'Crumbs', thought the boy, who was going to Scotland in the holidays, 'if they work on chub, what about salmon?' The enormity and ambition of this thought stunned him. For a moment he became still in reverie. A picture then floated into his mind of a triumphal return to the grown-ups at the shooting lodge with the 'King of Fish' in his arms. It was all quite clear and obvious — he knew it could be done.

In Scotland, at the mouth of the Sula river, a seal's head rose above the surface of the salt waters of the sea. The seal blew and sighed after his dive and looked about with large and filmy eyes. His whiskers dripped and steamed with the warmth of his breath on the cold dawn air. It was the middle of July on the West coast, the run of small one sea-winter salmon, which they call grilse, was on, and they, together with a few two sea-winter salmon, were entering the river on the flood tide. The seal had killed two, taking a bite from the swimming fish which then wobbled on erratically to fall away, sink and die, to the delight of crabs and lobster which feasted on the rich pink flesh. Other salmon, alarmed by the thudding shocks of the chase, shot forward in powerful upriver flight into the Sea Pool. The seal would not follow into the fresh peaty water and turned away to swim to Seal Island in the Sound. He hauled himself out onto the rocks to sleep and bask in the rising sun.

Old Donald saw a silver grilse leap in Sea Pool as he pushed his bicycle along the path beside the river and then a second fish of about 10 lb showed at the neck of the pool as it searched the way upstream. The old man nodded to himself with approval; it had always been so, spring tides on the flood brought in the fish, and if there was a spate as well, so much the better, for there would be no holding them for four or five miles in one go. Donald hitched the mail bag higher on his shoulder and continued up the valley to Shiel Lodge. He always walked up the valley to see the deer, a grouse or two and sometimes a blackcock in the field by the silver birches. He never saw much if he rode up the valley to deliver the letters, for his bicycle squeeked and grated, he had his head down, and, anyway, it was too much of a pull. Perhaps this afternoon he would have an hour or two on the river himself at Shiel Lodge if the tenants didn't mind.

For the boy the first day of the Scottish holiday had passed in a rush of activities. He had seen a deer before breakfast and a red squirrel had been chased up a tree by a dog. He went to the moor with the guns, but rain stopped the shoot at lunch time when the party returned to the house. The rain continued and the river rose in the late afternoon. Brown trout tucked themselves under the banks to escape the pressure of the peaty water and were passed by salmon and sea trout on their way upstream. Some travelling fish leaped with joy as each new pool was entered on their spawning run, others jumped to knock off the sea lice clinging with tiny suckers to their flanks.

Later the rain ceased and, having escaped from the house, the boy sat on a stump beside the river and watched the surface of the waters, his chin cupped in his hand. All the fish he saw seemed large to him, even the smaller sea trout which were called finnock in that part. There was too much water now, he was sure of that. Grandpa always said you had to wait for a spate to drop a bit. Perhaps it would be all right in the morning. Pity Grandpa wasn't here; he would know what to do to catch a salmon. Still, he had the chub fly.

The thought of the fly sent him scurrying home to prepare for fishing in the morning. He would have a go with the fly, give it a swim, as he had heard a keeper say. His rod really did not look strong enough and even his best leader hardly seemed up to the envisaged task, and as for the reel, it only had twenty-five yards of line upon it. He pulled off all the line and stretched it out behind the house; it really wasn't enough. He was certain salmon fishers had more line upon their reels, eighty or ninety yards he had heard some say. What about joining on the mackerel spinning line? Thirty pounds breaking strain was sure to be enough. He added twenty yards of this, joining the two sections with a bulky blood knot. All was ready for the morning and if he caught a fish he would land it somehow, by beaching, or grab it around the knuckle of the tail, or with his fingers in the gills. It could be done. The boy's breath came a little faster at the thought. He didn't eat much supper nor sleep too well that night.

The black fly swung on the current across the pool to hang below the rock on which the boy was crouched. It would not sink properly being too bushy. Fish were there without doubt; he had seen two salmon leap below the rock to crash down with such a splash that he felt even more doubtful of his tackle, and he was having difficulty in casting 'down and across' against the upstream wind which pushed at the downstream water flow and made great waves. He tried again during a lull. Out went the cast across the river and, as he raised his rod a little to retrieve, a gust of wind caught the line, whisking it upstream, causing the fly to scuttle over the surface of the rough, black water. A humping, sweeping, shining black-backed curve of salmon intercepted the skidding fly and took it down. The boy let out a shout, the short, sharp sound ejected from him without thought. The rod bent, the reel screeched, the line accelerated fast, and then he jumped — all the silver length and beauty of him. There was a chance, he knew there was a chance; the pool was not large, perhaps with twenty-five yards of line ....

But what about the knot to the mackerel backing? He mustn't let it go that far. The salmon came back below the boy, who held the rod with trembling arms, all of him shook and his legs were weak. He shifted to ease his knees indented by the rock and in moving pulled the salmon off balance in the water current. The fish shot off downstream, out of the pool and down through the rapids. The boy followed as best he could, stumbling over rocks. The fly line was out, the knot, thank goodness, passed through the rings without jamming and the mackerel line now took the strain. The boy came level with the fish again and reeled in as far as the mackerel knot 'The knot! The bloody knot!' the boy called out in sobbing despair, the knot would not come back through the top ring and the salmon was coming close to him.

'Eh, laddie, ye're in a turrible finckle', said the slow and kindly voice of Donald of the Mail, 'but he's almost done, slack off a wee bitty.' The old man had heard the crying shout as he pushed his bicycle along the nearby road and now, beside the boy, he gently took the sagging line between his rough and calloused fingers. The salmon was done. Donald drew on the line, beached the fish and pushed it firmly up the shelving sandy bank. 'Dap him on the haed', he told the boy, 'never let a fush be sufferin, yerr granfer would'na like ut'.

The postman removed the fly from the salmon's mouth and turned it over in his thick strong fingers. 'A mite fuzzy maybe, but ye never noo wi' saumon.'

II
SEA TROUT

10 Knowledge of the fish

Life history

During the third week of October 1986 grey curtains of drifting rain crossed the windy slopes of Dartmoor cloaking the purple heather-covered hills. A day later a heavy spate came down the river Tavy, which runs off the south western slopes to discharge its peaty water into the sea at Plymouth. Before this there had been little rain since 13 September; in consequence late-running salmon and peal, as we call sea trout in the south west, had been held up in the lower reaches of the river and in the estuary. In Tavistock there is a weir across the Tavy with a fish pass at one end; this pass is a simple one of a single, intermediate level between the weir pool and the river above. Salmon ascend to the upper river by leaping into the intermediate level and then swimming hard over three ascending steps to continue their upstream spawning run. At times the flow is too strong down the steps, and they wait in the turbulent depths of the level for the current to reduce.

Sea trout also use this pass, but when the spate is heavy they prefer to jump the 4 ft high gap between the water level of the weir pool and the river above, struggling momentarily on the cill at the top before an arrow on the water surface, at once swept away, marks their path upstream. Many fall back and have to try a second time. Peal may be seen in the white, frothing water of the weir pool, for a second or two as they poke their dark heads above the foam to take a look at the obstacle in their path, before they leap for the unknown water above.

Sea trout and salmon must have great courage. Peal of all sizes from ten slim ounces to several pounds of pent up leaping power run the course. A delayed autumn spate is one of the few chances the layman has to see the peal; he does not notice or even look for them in summer by day, certainly not by night, and the only other period when they may be seen by those who do not fish is whilst spawning in the streams of the high moor, which is out of reasonable walking distance for the majority.

To the angler the weir reveals many secrets: the number of school peal, the little ones, will indicate lean or plentiful seasons to come; 3 and 4-pounders are not uncommon, and the number of them may astonish the man who failed to catch one of this size in August. Then there are the monsters of 6, 7 and 8 or more pounds, but one is hard put to distinguish whether these are large sea trout or small salmon in the few airborne seconds. Very small fingerlings attempt the leap without success, and the watcher wonders whether they are brown trout or little peal.

116 *This speed of tail movement creates a spray as sea trout jump for the cill of Tavistock weir.*

Well, the fact is that, other than salmon, they are all trout. The difference between the brownie and the peal (finnock for small sea trout in Scotland; sewin for all sizes in Wales), other than colour variations, is one of habit. Sea trout migrate to the sea to feed at times in their life cycle, and brown trout do not. That is all. A peal is a migratory brown trout. On the gravel beds of the moorland streams and in the upper reaches of other rivers, including the chalk streams, the sea trout spawn in the second half of November and in December, cutting a redd where the female lays her eggs, which are at once fertilized by the shed milt of the male. If the water is low they may be watched in the same areas as the salmon. After about two months, depending upon the water temperature, the eggs hatch out and out comes an alevin with a suspended yolk sac, which sustains the fish for about one month. The alevin then becomes free feeding and is known as a fry. Dark bars of grey appear along its flanks after a while and it is then called a parr, as also is the salmon. The parr may stay in the river for two or three years, living and competing for food with the brown trout, before migrating to the sea in late spring as a smolt, by which time it has become silver in colour.

The first three sea trout I caught in my life weighed 7 oz each — they were smolts attempting to migrate to the sea and probably 6 or 7 years old. So long an initial freshwater period is exceptional. It happened in this way. In 1943 the newly constructed dam blocking the South Teign, a sea trout river on Dartmoor, was closed to create Fernworthy reservoir. Sea trout could not ascend the granite wall to reach the upper streams to spawn. When the river was shut off there were clearly sea trout redds above the obstruction. The eggs hatched and the little peal fed and stayed thereafter in the reservoir until they eventually died out.

On 3 September 1949 I caught one of these peal from a boat, together with four small brown trout, on a Peter Ross. The following year on 20 April 1950 I caught another and, more interesting, on 22 April, two days later, a third in the granite pool below the dam. The final fish was a silver sea trout smolt migrating down river at the correct time; it weighed 7 oz and fell to a Peter Ross. I have no doubt, from recent experiences with Fernworthy-stocked rainbows, that that it had escaped over the dam in the spring overflow resulting from winter rainfall. I saw no more of them in ensuing seasons.

From smolt to peal

The smolt will put on 5 or 6 oz in weight in the sea in four months and may then return as a school peal in July, August or September, or it may remain in the sea for a year or longer. If it does return in the same season as its first marine excursion it may spawn as a fish of 10 or 12 oz., certainly many of these little sea trout reach the spawning beds but, unlike salmon after spawning, they do not die but return to the sea.

How long they spend at sea varies, but it is my view that if they leave the river in January or February they are likely to come back into fresh water in July or August as peal weighing about 20 oz. These 1 lb-plus fish will spawn and return to the sea as kelts, recover themselves and again run up to spawn, this time weighing two or more pounds. On their journey down the river after spawning the sea trout kelts will sometimes take the lures of early season salmon anglers—this has happened to me a number of times and, of course, these spent fish must be returned.

Sea trout enter our rivers from March onwards. From my own observation the early runs of heavy fish, the 5 lb-plus specimens, of which one is lucky to catch half a dozen in a lifetime, enter in March and April. May sees an influx of those in the region of 3 or 4 lb — again in small numbers, but there are more of them than the earlier specimens. The final week of June and then July and August is the time of the 1–2-pounders which mingle with the school peal. These schedules are just a guide to months and weights; large sea trout are not confined solely to March and April— they enter at any time thereafter but only in small numbers. I don't know exactly to what age a sea trout will live, but a span of two or three juvenile river years, followed by three years oscillating between sea and river with two or three spawnings is a supportable assumption based on the numbers caught at different weights. Of course some peal live longer, but the percentage of the whole to survive each spawning must steadily decrease.

Sea trout lies

Sea trout will run up river by night and day in a spate. In low water I have not observed them running by day, but there is no doubt that they move upstream in the dark when, although you cannot see them, you can hear the splashes and slaps as they cross the stones of shallow runs. The best way to discover sea trout in the summer is to climb a tree or look down into the river from a high bank to spot them through polaroid spectacles. They usually lie in small groups on the riverbed - grey shadows which scarcely move until one, through some irritation, twists, turns and shows a silver flank, perhaps swimming in a wide circle before returning to the original shoal. One year there will be only small groups, but the next you may see 60 or 70 within a river length of a hundred yards. The other method of establishing their occupation of a pool is to watch at dusk — other than on a cold evening peal almost always jump straight into the air, splash, and arrow across the pool just lifting the surface film.

Although you may spy out sea trout by day, they will not necessarily remain in the same place at night and even if they do, and you cannot be certain of the fact unless they jump, they may not be in a lie from which they will readily come to the fly. Places where sea trout show are not necessarily those where they take. The lies they occupy at night and from which they will take a fly alter with water height, but not to the same extent as salmon, for peal fishing is not good in high water. On the whole they tend to spend the daylight hours in deeper water than they will occupy from dusk onwards. It is my experience that their positions usually change as soon as night falls. All the same a daytime reconnaissance will let you know whether the fish are in the pool.

The best sea-trout pools have a long, deep glide gradually shallowing out towards the run-off. If the side from which you are to fish is shallow and the far side is deep and beneath trees and bushes, and all this is towards the tail of a pool 100 yd long, you will very likely be looking at an excellent piece of water. It is always better to cast from shallow water into deep. If you stand over the deep side of the pool you will be much more visible to the fish beneath your feet, and you will be attempting to land your catch in the immediate vicinity of the shoal. Additionally, you will be silhouetted against the sky. Sea trout will move into fast shallow water in hot weather, no doubt the extra flow brings them a better supply of oxygen; in such runs they may be caught at times, but rapids are not the most productive areas.

As with salmon, the sea trout likes to lie in front of something: stones and boulders are favoured, as is the upward shelving gravel at the pool run-off; but the two most productive lies I know are short trenches in the riverbed. These places, no more than 6 or 7 ft long and a yard wide, are about 2 ft deeper than the river bed on either flank. Both of these catching troughs are at the tail of a long, gliding pool, with a deep, central daytime holding area.

River feeding

Whilst one can say with certainty that salmon do not feed in fresh water, it is unwise to apply this to sea trout. I have lain on the bank at times for an hour or two to watch the fish - they do not move much, but very occasionally I have seen one rise to the surface to take a fly, and there is no doubt that, at times, they may be taken on the dry fly by day, by which I mean the middle of the day, not just at dusk. I have seen many instances of this in rivers: a friend took one of 1 lb 12 oz. on a No. 16 Black Gnat. I have had them on a No. 12 Red

Sedge as well and a doctor I know took three or four on a mayfly, yellow in colour, from the river Frome one afternoon in a wet gale. But these are isolated instances; on the whole they do not feed to the extent that they intend to maintain their body weight or put on additional ounces on their return from the sea. The cleaning and examination of the stomach contents of several sea trout after a night's fishing will not take long — there is usually nothing to see in the empty white gut.

Visual capacity of sea trout

What is the visual capacity of sea trout? Do they see in colour? How well at night, and why are they able to see a black fly in the darkest hours? It seems rational that as brown trout see in colour, and this has been established that sea trout are also able to distinguish the colours of the spectrum, although some shades better than others. But perhaps colour is not so important in the dark as silhouette and a bright gleam — thus black and silver find a place in many sea trout fly dressings for use in the dark, and red is added by day.

The ability of sea trout to see at night better than ourselves is due to the fuller use they make of the available light. In the human eye the light enters and travels through the lens, which focuses it on the retina, any excess light being reduced by a contraction of the iris. The sea trout takes matters a stage further. Behind their retina is a mirror, the tapetum, composed of iridocyte cells containing crystals of silver-coloured guanine. This mirror reflects the light back through the retina in a double pass. In effect, the light is used twice.

The sea trout does not have an iris, as the human, to control light entering the eye, and thus by day too much light may cause reflections to shoot about inside their eye. Fish control this problem with a pigment that dulls the mirror by day but clears from the tapetum by night or in conditions of poor light.

You may fish for peal on the darkest night in the full confidence that he is able to see a great deal more than yourself when close to the fly, but he may not be able to see it from any marked distance if the water is turbid. Nevertheless, a fat tube fly on a treble hook will set up a disturbance in the smooth glides, since it moves at a speed different from that of the water. It seems likely that the fish is able to detect these disturbances and thus a treble-hooked fly is the best choice in coloured water as a spate commences to recede. Neither of these factors, vision and sensitivity, does away with the desirability of knowing almost exactly the position of your quarry. Once again knowledge of lies is of the utmost importance.

Distinguishing sea trout from salmon

It is necessary that the angler distinguish between large sea trout and small salmon, not only for his own satisfaction but because their open seasons may not be the same in a river in England and Wales. The sea trout season on many rivers opens several weeks after salmon fishing commences. As the early part of the season is the time when most of the large sea trout enter it is possible to take a sea trout of 7 or 8 lb in early March when the season does not open until the fifteenth of that month. Grilse

of 4–5 lb are common in summer, and sea trout of that size, whilst not common, are not remarkable. It is essential that one knows the distinguishing features:

The tail—in the salmon, particularly grilse, the trailing edge of the tail is concave. In a sea trout it is square.

The eye—in the salmon the rear edge of the eye is level with the rear end of the maxillary bone. In the sea trout the rear of the eye is forward of the end of the maxillary bone.

The scales—a sea trout's scales at once appear smaller and more numerous than those of the salmon when he is on the bank, and there are usually more dark spots on the flank. A scale count taking a row from the rear of the adipose fin forward to the lateral line will be 10–12 for salmon and 13–15 for sea trout.

In general a large sea trout is a chunkier looking fish than a grilse, the head is shorter and the top of the shoulder, where it meets the skull, is almost hunched. A grilse has a longer head, particularly the cock fish.

117 *Four sea trout to 6½ lb. River Test. Testwood Pool, Redbridge to Tony Allen and Brian Parker, head river keeper on Bossington Estate, Stockbridge. 2 in. black streamer fly. Top fish has gill cover torn by nets. Bottom fish has net marks on flanks. Note square tails, forward eye and small scales.*

118 *Four salmon. No. 4 single-hooked*
Thunder & Lightning, to Tony Allen from
River Test at Broadlands. Note concave
tails and larger scales.

119 *Grilse, sea trout or hybrid? A scale count revealed the fish to be a grilse despite almost square tail. Eye should be farther forward if a sea trout.*

Disease and parasites

Sea trout are subject to UDN but not to the same extent as salmon. No doubt this is because the majority arrive from June onwards when the water has warmed — UDN seems to be a disease which is more prevalent in cold water. Bad outbreaks have occurred in the past amongst the 2 and 3-pounders of late April and early May, but thereafter diseased sea trout are uncommon. Sea lice will be found on sea trout fresh run from tidal waters, and these parasites are an indication of the distances the fish are capable of running upstream on entering the river. A friend of mine caught an $8\frac{1}{2}$ lb sea trout on a fly whilst salmon fishing in the first week of June 15 miles from salt water; the fish had sea lice, and these usually fall off after 48 hours in the river. Few fish run so far in so short a time. Upstream migration of 30 miles may normally take three or four months if the fish leaves the sea in mid-summer. Although I have found gill maggots in salmon kelts, and in salmon which have been in the river for three or four months but have not spawned, I have not found these parasites in the gills of sea trout. I have found white worms in their stomachs on rare occasions.

11 Sea trout equipment

Fly-rods

Sea trout rods are single-handed, and for river fishing may be of 9–10 ft in length. A rod for night use, the majority of our fishing, needs to deal with fish of up to 4 or 5 lb which will be taken on a leader of 8–10 lb breaking strain. As the angler will frequently wade, and the rod thus be closer to the water level than if he were on the bank, the rod should be about 9 ft to give good command of the river in casting and to hold as much line as possible above the water when playing a fish. Long casting is not a regular necessity, but even so a stiff rod is desirable to punch a line into the wind. A rod of soft action should be avoided.

For boat fishing a rod of 11 ft is better than one of 9 or 10 ft. The greater height will enable the caster to retrieve his bob fly across the surface of the loch. For daytime river fishing fine nylon will be required; this would be snapped by a stiff rod when playing or hooking a sea trout. Use a rod of about 9 ft in length with an easy action. Your ordinary dry-fly river trout rod is all that is required, and this will probably take a No. 6 line.

Particular attention should be paid to the reel mounting on all sea trout rods. Those with a butt cap and sliding or screw ring to hold the reel are not suitable, for the reel will press against the angler's coat, with involuntary braking as a result, and there will be no support to the wrist. A better arrangement is the fixed screw grip with a rubber button behind the reel, but this by itself is not ideal because the button only extends by 1 in. behind the back of the rim of the reel. In Hardy De Luxe rods over 9 ft in length the rubber button may be removed and a 4 in. screw-in extension fitted. Again this is not entirely satisfactory because 4 in. is too long a butt extension, and the fly-line tends to loop around it when casting. A 2 in. extension is ideal and used to be available from the manufacturers — as this is no longer the case it would not be difficult to make one or cut down the 4 in. model. The 10 ft impregnated, split-cane Sea Trout Special has a 2 in. built-in extension behind the reel fitting — this is ideal, but the rod is too heavy for some anglers.

As with salmon fly-rods we have three materials from which to choose.

Split cane

The 10 ft split-cane rod mentioned above is suitable in all respects but one — its weight of 9¼ oz. A night of steady casting with such a rod may cramp the hand and be beyond the physical capacity of many. All the same it is the right length for river fishing at night and is also suitable for use in a boat.

Fibreglass

Many anglers will find their ordinary still water or reservoir trout rods perfectly adequate for sea trout if the length of the rod is between 9 and 10 ft and sufficiently stiff to warrant a No. 7 or No. 8 line. The disadvantage of fibreglass is the unavoidable fat diameter of the tube, which produces considerable air resistance when casting against the wind — all the same, fibreglass is a good choice for the river since a rod as described will have plenty of power and be reasonably light in weight.

Carbon fibre

A 10 ft carbon fibre rod is ideal for night fishing in the river, and will weigh in the region of 4–5 oz., depending on its stiffness, which will be matched to the AFTM line rating. The carbon fibre rod is thin in the tube compared with fibreglass, and is thus less tiring in use; particularly it is more efficient in casting against the wind.

A long rod is a necessity for boat fishing to enable the bob fly and a dropper to be scuttled over the water surface on the retrieve. You will find 10 ft adequate but 11 ft is very much better; at this length carbon fibre is essential in a single-handed rod.

Fly-reels

As advised in Chapter 3, a large simple reel is better than a small, complicated multiplier. Fly-lines of AFTM No. 7 and No. 8 will be in use to match the rods described. These lines may be accommodated on reels of $3\frac{5}{8}$ in., which is a spool diameter to recover line rapidly — provided the spool is full. There is a considerable choice of makes.

I have two different reels in use in this size: the Leeda graphite Dragonfly 100 is light in weight at $4\frac{1}{2}$ oz.; the Hardy Marquis No. 8/9 costs about twice as much as the Dragonfly, is made of aluminium with a nickel-plated line guard and weighs $5\frac{3}{4}$ oz.

The Marquis is rather shiny on one side for night use. Both these reels have adjustable drags, and spare spools may be fitted through a central release catch. Both are rated to accommodate line weight above those we intend to use — in other words they have a greater line volume capacity than is required for No. 7 and No. 8 lines. This is desirable, for not only will the line be recovered more quickly by the larger diameter drum, but they will take more backing.

Whilst the largest Hardy Perfect of $3\frac{5}{8}$ in. diameter is too small in the latest edition for the No. 9 lines required in salmon fishing, it will take No. 7 and No. 8 double-tapered floating lines for sea trout, and 60 yd of 18 lb braided Dacron backing. It is a delightful dark-coloured reel, and unlike older examples the reel of today has interchangeable spools in the right-hand wind models, but not those winding on the left.

Fly-lines

The majority of time spent night fishing will be with a floating line, and this will also be used from a boat. There is little need for sinking lines for these may cause the fly to catch on the riverbed in low water, and summer levels are when most of our fishing will take place. If a need is felt for a sinking line it would be best to purchase a slow sinker rather than a sink tip line. Sink tips are satisfactory for salmon fishing by day in a full river but in quiet conditions by night the tip tends to hit the water at the end of the cast with more impact than the floating section. This action is due to the different specific gravities of the two sections of the line — the lightweight floating part and the more dense tip.

Few long casts are necessary at night. The 25 yd throw is an unlikely requirement, casts of 10 or 15 yd being more normal. In consequence, the length of line held in the air outside the rod tip when false casting is likely to be short, and will thus not weigh much. To balance the rod on short casts be sure to use the line weight recommended by the manufacturer or even the next heavier. If the rod is rated at No. 7/8 use the No. 8 in a small river. Only in a wide river on such a rod go to the No. 7.

The colour of the fly-line is important. It is a great help to be able to see the line at night on the dark surface of the water. The speed of drift of the line, the position of the fly, the lie of a sea trout plucking at the fly without a full take, will be readily located if the line is white and there is the smallest glimmer of light in the sky. I have advised against white fly-lines in salmon fishing on the basis that they are more visible on the water by day and scare fish if undesirable false casts are made. I do not believe that the false cast/white line problem applies in the dark. Even so, keep false casts to a minimum to reduce the likelihood of leader tangles. The Scientific Angler's Air-Cel Supreme double-taper floating fly-line is ivory white (do not purchase by mistake the tan colour that is also marketed under the Supreme classification). The Hardy Dry Fly is ice blue, shows up well and is in the medium price range. Both of these lines are available in double taper and weight

forward — choose the double taper, not only for economy but also for roll casts. For a slow-sinking line the Scientific Angler's Wet Cel 1 and the Hardy Wet Fly 1 are both made in a medium green colour that is well-suited for a sinking line.

Leaders

Good turnover of the line and leader is essential both by day and night. Particularly is this so when casting upstream; in this direction the current will not straighten a leader that lands in coils on the water. It is therefore necessary to use a tapered leader to continue the tapering of the line, and the leader should not be over long. A 3 yd leader with a thick butt is sufficient — a greater length is not necessary and will fail to cut into an opposing wind. Do not fish fine at night. A point of less than 8 lb test is undesirable, and in circumstances where sea trout of 5 lb are expected, or a grilse at sunset, it would be better to choose 10 lb. Manufactured knotless tapered leaders are not necessary in the dark; it is cheaper to make your own tapered leader from Platil Strong monofilament as follows:

Knot a 1 yd butt of 20 lb test with a blood knot to a centre section of 13 lb, which should be blood knotted to a point of 1 yd of 10.5 lb or 8.5 lb. You may tie a blood bight loop at the end of the butt section for attachment to the fly-line, but a better method of attaching the leader to the fly-line is to needle knot 1 ft of 20 lb nylon to the fly-line and blood knot this to the leader butt. The needle knot method has two advantages: your fly will not catch on the line/leader junction knot when false

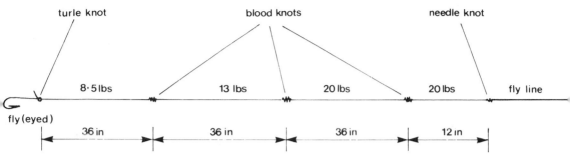

120 *A homemade tapered leader. Made of Platil Strong this leader is ideal for night sea trout fishing. The 8.5 lb point could be replaced by 10 lb if heavy fish are expected. A tucked half blood knot would be used to attach a tube fly.*

casting, and you may wind the junction through the top ring of the rod in the dark, or let it run out, without being held up. This second reason is sufficient to require the use of the needle knot arrangement at all times, particularly if the leader is 9 ft long and fished off a 9 ft rod. To draw the fish close enough to be netted when wading in the dark will almost certainly entail winding the line/leader junction up to the top ring of a short rod. If this point is drawn through the top ring (and you cannot see when this is about to happen in the dark), a smashed hook hold or leader may result if the fish again swims off and a bulky knot, such as the Sheet Bend, has been used; it may stick when drawn up to the inside of the top ring. A needle knot will slide in and out without jamming.

Do not use droppers at night. A single fly creates few tangles and there is no free fly to catch in the meshes when netting a fish. Droppers catch fish for the skilled caster, but until one is thoroughly competent in handling tackle in the

river, in the dark, more time will be lost in sorting out tangles than is worthwhile.

Fishing by day for school peal, finnock or small sewin is a delicate matter, requiring a careful stalk, smooth wading, accurate casts, no splash and as little line and leader shadow as possible on the river bed. A trout rod of 9 ft in length is suitable with a No. 5 or No. 6 line and a 9 ft knotless tapered leader without droppers. You should not make your own leader from reducing sections knotted together: the knots will produce line shadow and disturbance on the water surface. Knotless tapered leaders are marketed by Normark, Hardy, Leeda Platil and others. The point has to be fine or the peal will be scared, anything thicker than seven thousandths of an inch, being rated at 4X and 4 lb will be rejected. A 5X rating of 3 lb test would be better. Too fine for peace of mind, but there is no alternative if you want a take.

Nets

The Gye-type net with a sliding shaft, carried on a sling on the back, is too clumsy for use in the dark. Frequent unslinging and replacement for fish of around the 1 lb mark would be taking a sledgehammer to crack a nut. Folding

121 *Bass, next to the body, and net on dog clip.*

arm-type nets are not reliable for two reasons: the arms may fail to open and click into place if their tips become entangled in the net meshes and, secondly, a large sea trout may be partially supported on the cord joining the arms, the cord will then sag and the peal slide out. Choose a rigid metal bowframe net with a 20 in. wide hinged frame. This will take anything up to 7 lb but will not be unwieldy for small sea trout. The handle should not be telescopic; a length of shaft of 32 in. is ideal to act as a short, wading probe and depth gauge. If the hand on the hinge touches the water, as you feel along the river bed, the water is just about to run over the top of thigh boots which are also in the region of 32 in. from sole to top. The bowframe should be white or silver to show up in the dark — quite the opposite of a trout- or salmon-net frame which should be camouflaged by green or black paint for daytime use.

Most nets have a spring hook just behind the hinge. This is intended to hook onto the trouser belt or a ring on a fishing coat, but the angler may not wear a coat and the hook is not easy to pull off the trousers belt. A better arrangement is to suspend a spring clip, of the type found on a dog lead, 4 or 5 in. below the belt. Hardy's used to market a very handsome example in leather and brass, but the dog-type will do and this readily gives up the net, which may then be flipped up into the open-locked position.

Miscellaneous equipment

The bass

A 16 in. x 16 in. bass will hold three sea trout up to 2 lb in weight. When wading, the bass should be next to the body and also clipped to the dog clip. This net/bass arrangement enables the angler to net and store fish whilst in the river without needing to take each sea trout to the bank — such movements disturb the pool.

The priest

Do not attach the priest to the dog clip, for there will not be sufficient reach to knock a fish on the head whilst still in the net, and if unclipped the priest may be dropped into the river. Instead have the priest on a loop of cord around your neck and of a length that will enable you to keep it in your trousers pocket.

The scissors

The small Swiss army knife which has a single blade, a pair of tweezers and scissors, may be suspended on a thin cord around the neck to hang just above waist level if tucked inside the front of the coat or fishing waistcoat. The scissors are a boon in cutting nylon to make or repair leaders. Be sure to choose the model that has a lanyard shackle to take the suspending cord.

Waders

Choose waders with cleated rubber soles. Metal-studded boots clatter under water on the rocks of the river bed and may scare fish. At night you must move like a ghost — no vibrations.

Torch

Use a small torch that may be held in a manner that leaves the hands free to tie knots. Some models may be clipped to a pocket on the front of the jacket and others are of a size and shape which may be held in the mouth. I tend to dribble with a torch between my teeth: instead I place a small flat model between my thighs as I kneel on the ground to work on tackle. There is a useful torch called the Flexy Spot from Pegley-Davies   this has a multipurpose attachment clip and a spot light on a flexible neck.

Fly boxes

Two boxes are required: one with compartments to hold daytime dry flies, and the other for night use. The best dry fly box that I know is made in aluminium by Wheatley — mine has had a thorough testing over 40 years, during which span it has acquired the patina of old silver. The night box must take both single-hooked flies and treble-hooked tubes — the clipped variety does not fulfil both needs. Choose a very simple flat foam-lined box for wet flies and tubes, all the hooks, both single and treble, may be pressed into the foam sides. Such a box will not cost more than a pound or two, which is no great loss if it is mislaid in the dark. A red plastic box of this type comes free with the Leeda HI-TEC Gallion Floating fly line, which is inexpensive, green and satisfactory for day fishing. If you wish to fish a surface dry fly in the dark, store two or three, already waterproofed, in the plastic cylinder in which 35 mm films are sold.

Sink mix

When fishing wet fly at night your leader must sink below the surface on the first cast. It will not do this at once unless you take the trouble to wipe it in advance with a de-greaser. Dry nylon that has been handled will float. Proprietary sinking compounds are available, but the simplest arrangment is to take a 6 in. square of old shirt tail, wet it, sprinkle with Fuller's Earth (from Boots the Chemists) and add a few drops of dish wash liquid. The wet cloth may be placed in a film spool cylinder of a different colour from the dry flies.

Midge repellant

This is essential. A jelly or aerosol spray is better than cream which will find its way, via your hands, onto the leader, causing it to float. Boots market their insect repellant gel - one application at dusk will last the night.

Game bag

Take a game bag to the river to establish a base site in the middle of the beat. This bag should hold a raincoat, coffee flask and sandwiches, spare tackle and an extra torch, plastic bags, string and spare clothing. Include two plastic bin sacks in which the game bag, and anything else, may be kept dry if it rains. The plastic bags will hold sea trout when these are tipped out of the bass - if they are not covered with polythene, but just left on the wet grass, they will attract hungry slugs. It is unpleasant to pick up both peal and slug, and hard to remove the slime from your hand.

Fly floatant

Many types are available as liquids or aerosol sprays. The best is Richard Walker's Supafloat. Tie the dry fly to the leader, push the fly into the neck of the bottle (this may sound a trifle agricultural but does no harm), cover the opening with your thumb and give a couple of shakes, blow off and allow to dry completely before use. As an alternative, before tying to the leader, and by day in advance of a night at the river, push the eye of the fly and the body down into the bottle neck, the hook will catch over the rim, close with the thumb, shake, remove, blow off and dry.

Clothing

It is possible to calculate from a combination of height and distance the point at which an above surface object, the fisherman, will be visible to a sea trout at a known depth. But the angler does not know the precise position or the exact depth of all the peal in his area in the night. The man who keeps low, or is wading, may be out of the field of view of the peal — but he cannot count on it! Even if the peal is unable to see you, sombre clothing and dull-coloured headwear will have the correct effect on the angler — he will be aware that he must be stealthy.

During warm summer nights wear a dark green sweater, a dull hat or cap and a brown shirt. A sunburned face and hands (I always worry about white skinned hands casting at head height), and a dark-coloured rod with a reel which does not have bright chromium plated parts, will turn a careful peal fisher into a phantom fading into the night. It is all a matter of attitude to the job in hand. If fish cannot hear you — still keep quiet; if fish cannot see you — still be camouflaged. Peal can detect vibration — don't jump down the river-bank. Imagine yourself to be a burglar stealing a fish from the river, and dress accordingly.

Sea trout flies

Night

The first 'sea trout' I caught at night was on 7th June 1969. I had caught the fish by day from a boat in the early 1950s in Scotland, but at night — No. They just didn't come my way. This was largely lack of opportunity but there was also something wrong, I didn't know what it was and there was no one to teach me. The first 'sea trout' came about as follows in a moorland river.

> *7 June. Low water. SE wind. Didn't fish until after dinner. Took trout rod to Stoney Pool at 9.15 pm. Wind dropped to a gentle breeze. Salmon and sea trout moved at dusk. 2¾ lb trout! 10.30 pm at top of pool to a small Black Pennell. Started to fish when almost dark. The chap with the white Ford Taunus estate car commenced fishing as I left at 11 pm. Said he took most of his sea trout in the tail of the pool, and had taken two salmon at the top, all at night on large sea trout flies on 8 lb nylon. Often fished through the night and said dawn was a good time for salmon.*

So, the first 'sea trout' did not break the night time duck, although I was sure I had one on when playing the fish, for on the 8 ft 6 in. CC de France split cane it put up an athletic battle. The two factors that accounted for my failure up to that time are contained in the diary entry: fishing the head of the pool instead of the tail, and using a 'small' Black Pennell. If I had used a large Black Pennell and fished the run-off success would have been mine at night long before 7 June 1969.

With sea trout flies for night fishing there is little doubt that size is more important than colour. Even after 1969 I persisted with standard patterns on No. 12 hooks - Peter Ross, Mallard & Claret, Grouse & Red and others of that type. If the peal were really on the go a few would come my way — but not in either spectacular numbers or remarkable sizes. I had not yet turned the key in the lock — when the key did turn it was the result of talking to a local who fished the river Teign. He showed me his flies: they were enormous by my standards. Whacking great tandem-hooked lures 1½ in. or more in length in blue and silver. He cast them upstream and down; up under the bankside bushes on the far side and down into the clear open water. He caught peal. Large ones. My mouth watered and my eyes popped out. He was so casual about it all, his equipment was ancient, the rod unvarnished and the fly-line cracked; even his dog had seen better days. But he turned the key and I was grateful.

My armoury now is very simple for night sub-surface fishing — just four flies. Two of these are treble-hooked socketed tubes and two are singles. It is better for the beginner to start with a single hook for they are unlikely to tangle on the leader, as may happen with a treble.

Black lure

This is dressed on a single No. 8 hook, which must be of very good quality. If the water is cloudy the size may be increased to No. 6. It is a fly to be fished more than any other, particularly on dark nights and in low water. If the peal have been in the river for three or four weeks and are becoming stale it does better than a silver-bodied fly. The dressing is as follows:

Hook: Mustad Viking 9672. Size No.
            8, forged, hollow point, down
            eye, extra long shank
Body: Black floss
Rib: No. 14 oval silver tinsel
Throat: Black cock hackle
Wing: Two black cock hackles
Silk: Black Naples

Single hooks in salmon fishing are not
to be recommended, but the sea trout
has a softer mouth that allows better
penetration. It is not unusual to find the
point of this hook has gone through the
thickness of the snout of a sea trout to
the extent that it protrudes above the
nose and catches in the meshes of the
net. This eyed fly should be tied to the
leader with a Turle Knot, as should the
eyed Teal & Silver Blue that follows. If
this fly is tied on a No. 4 Loop Eye
Single Low Water Salmon hook with
an up eye it will be heavier than the No.
8 Black Lure and will fish closer to the
bottom, in fact it may catch on the
rocks in shallow water when fished off a
floating line. Particularly suited to the
deeper pool and fresh run sea trout.

Teal & Silver Blue
Hook: No. 4 Loop Eye Single Sal-
            mon up eye. The Sprite Hook
            is available from Veniard or
            Partridge Code 01 Single Wil-
            son No. 4 or 6
Body: Flat silver tinsel, ribbed fine
            oval silver
Throat: Blue hen hackle
Wing: Teal flank feathers
Silk: Black Naples

Socketed tube flies are fatter than flies
tied on single hooks, but unless there
is a socket the treble hook may turn
sideways and catch on the leader. The
night angler may be unaware that this

has happened and continue casting for
some time to no purpose. My two flies
are dressed on Veniard's type B socketed
1 in. tubes; the hook being a Partridge
No. 12 CS8 Sea Trout Treble. This
treble is out-pointed with a ringed eye
of large diameter to facilitate nylon
threading in the dark. The hook size
may appear small when compared with
the No. 8 used in the salmon tubes, but
it has a long shank and fishes well clear
of the tube body, which is slimmer,
carrying no lead wire or ribbing in the
dressing.

Alexandra tube
Tube: 1 in. type B Slipstream socketed
Hook: No. 12 Partridge CS8 outpoint
            treble
Tag: Scarlet floss
Body: Flat silver tinsel
Wing: Green peacock herl
Head: Black varnish
Silk: Black Naples

The wing is tied in sparsely around the
complete circumference of the head and
should reach to just beyond the treble
hook. Two jungle cock cheeks may be
added if desired. The Alexandra is for
general use but particularly comes into
its own in a medium water flow at the
end of a spate.

Silver Stoat's Tail
Finally we come to the Silver Stoat's
Tail. I cannot now remember why I first
tied this fly for sea trout, but it at
once became a favourite in moonlight
following this experience on the lower
Dart.

*24 August 1980. Started fishing tail
of The Manse 9.30 pm. A heavy fish
of about 5 lb (sea trout) showed in
the run off. No plucks or pulls. Went*

to extreme tail of Embankment Pool, a tiny dimple at the fly, in bright moonlight, showed a fish following. Next cast took a sea trout of two and a quarter pounds, 11.15 pm right in tail of glide. Went then to top of Embankment Glide and fished down under trees, casting to opposite bank in top fast run. Again a tiny dimple at the fly, followed next cast by sea trout 3¾ lb., landed at midnight. A small fish below this 30 minutes later. All fish in bright, cloudless, almost full moon on one inch Silver Stoat's Tail. This was a night on which almost no fish jumped and there were very few plucks and pulls.

Thinking about these events later I felt sure that the 'tiny dimple' at the fly — in fact it was about one foot behind — was made by the dorsal fin of the peal cutting the water film as the peal followed and inspected the lure.

The dressing is as follows:

Tube: 1 in. type B Slipstream socketed
Hook: No. 12 Partridge CS8 outpoint treble
Body: Flat silver tinsel
Wing: Two tufts of stoat's tail, one on each side of a length to reach the end of the tube
Head: Black varnish
Silk: Black Naples

No doubt the silver body glitters in the moonlight, and perhaps a certain amount of flash is caused by the black wings covering and then revealing the reflecting silver tube.

Do not tie more of these tubes than is needed for immediate use. Once off the spool, flat silver tinsel gradually oxidizes and fades. Wild stoats tails are all black at the tip; they are no longer readily available owing to the reduction in vermin control on many shoots. The keeper's gibbet is now rarely seen — if one is found and the line of suspended stoats are missing their tails you will know a fisherman has passed that way. Road casualties are my usual source — amputate the tail on a fence post with the pocket knife. After this surgery your fingers will smell to high heaven unless washed in a roadside puddle.

Dry fly

Now the dry fly at night. This is no more than a floating lure, it is not an imitation of any particular insect on which peal are feeding, for peal don't usually feed in fresh water. The lure works by creating a V-shaped ripple when cast down and across to skate back over the river surface until it hangs below the angler. I often fish a bucktail mayfly tied for me by Tony Allen — not because it is necessarily more attractive to the sea trout that any other large and bumbly fly, but because it appeals to me, and the bucktail is naturally buoyant. To have faith in the fly is half the battle, and as this mayfly has prominent wings it may, perhaps, awaken a youthful sea trout feeding memory.

Tony's dressing is as follows:

Hook: No. 8 Partridge Long Mayfly
Body: Yellow seal's fur ribbed fine gold wire
Front hackle: Blue dun
Palmered hackle: Blue dun
Tail: Three ginger cock whisks
Wing: Brown bucktail Split shaving brush tying

It would be worth trying a dapping fly such as the Loch Ordie or the Red Palmer.

Red Palmer

Hook: Size No. 10 Wilson up-eye

Body: Red seal's fur
Rib: Fine gold tinsel
Hackle: Red game hackles 'palmered' from the bend to the eye of the hook

Flies for day fishing

Few people fish for sea trout with the fly by day in rivers in low water because it is more productive to try for them at night. This does not mean that peal cannot be caught in sunshine and low water — but it is difficult not to scare this sensitive unpredictable fish. The practical side of the fishing will be covered later, and flies already suggested for the night will be put to use in high water.

In low water the most likely approach is to cast upstream with a fine leader and a small fly, dry or wet, or a nymph. As the upstream wet fly needs to sink a little, for sea trout remain close to the bottom, some lead should be incorporated in the dressing. The wet Black & Peacock Spider is worth a try on a No. 12 hook with a bronze peacock herl body and black hen's hackle: as I have said, wind a few turns of fine lead wire beneath the dressing.

Try a Pheasant Tail Nymph tied on a No. 12 hook. The weight will be provided by the tying material, fine copper wire, and the tail, body and humped thorax all come from six or eight fibres from the tail of a cock pheasant. In calm, bright, dry weather a dry fly should be small. A Black Gnat on a No. 16 hook is as good as anything else and need not have wings, just a black silk body and black cock hackle. Other flies to try are the Red Sedge and Wickham's Fancy. In rough weather by day, with a strong upstream wind to produce waves, the dry Black Gnat will be insignificant — use instead the Allen mayfly, well waterproofed with Supafloat.

Naturalist, writer, broadcaster and master of the upstream dry fly and the bare hook nymph, Oliver Kite, who died in 1968, described a fly he used on sea trout as follows:

I had brought with me a bit of old darning wool of some nondescript shade. Before I began fishing I put my little vice on my car boot, wired a hook, camouflaged the bright metal with an inch or two of this wool, wound tightly round. I gave this rude nymph a thorax of reindeer-hair. I also had a bare wired hook, Size 0, and I started fishing with that, so as to create the minimum disturbance.

His nymph was small, Size 0 being on the New Scale, is equal to No. 15 on the Old, or Redditch, Scale. On these two creations, the nymph and the reindeer thing, he took two sea trout by casting upstream, and lost a third. The fish weighed just under a pound in one case, and the scale was pulled down to 2 lb 13 oz. by the other.

12 Fly-fishing by night

Casting

If you cannot fish with competence by day do not go sea trout fishing with the fly at night. A casting error in daylight, resulting in a simple tangle, is seen at once and rectified. At night it is a different matter. the experienced caster in the dark will be able to detect almost at once, from a slight sound and movement variation of rod and line on the forward and back casts, if his tube fly has hooked back on itself, or on the fly line, or if a loop has formed in the leader. Not so the novice: he will continue casting, the tangle will worsen and in all probability the leader will require replacement. That, for him, may be a task of some moment, whilst it will be accomplished with speed and dexterity by the person who has fished for trout for a season or two.

This book does not set out to teach trout fishing or the methods of single-handed casting. It has to be assumed that experience in these fields has been acquired. All the same, there is a difference in casting in the dark, for greater care must be taken to ensure that tangles do not occur — this calls for concentration and alertness, coupled with competence in executing simple casts.

I have found that tangles are unlikely to arise if the forward and back casts are made in slightly different planes. By this I mean the creation of a slight elipse by the rod tip. If right-handed and fishing from the right bank downstream, take the lift-off back cast away a little to your right, that is downstream, and the forward throw, if brought directly over the head, will be clear. If fishing from the left bank take the lift-off back cast up and to the left, again bringing the forward cast straight overhead.

Tangles also arise from casting too quickly, allowing insufficient time for the fly-line and leader to straighten in the air behind the angler on the back cast before he starts the forward movement. I do not know why it is but people increase the speed of the rod movement at night and thus reduce the second or two which must be allowed for the line to extend over the bank behind. I do it at times when concentrating on the fish, and have to make an effort to slow down. If there is a whip-like crack in the air behind you the cause is either insufficient time allowed for the back cast to straighten, insufficient power to enable it to do so, or the rod has been taken too far back past the vertical before being stopped. These are easy matters to put right, provided you know what is wrong, and it is better to rectify faults during the day. To take someone sea trout fishing if he cannot cast well will only make him angry and frustrated at his own incompetence.

Judging the length of the cast is no problem for the experienced man. Provided he uses one rod for night fishing, and always a line of the same AFTM rating, he will be able to tell by the weight of line he is holding in the air outside the rod tip, and the coils in his hand to be shot through the rod rings on the forward cast, how far that cast will reach. He will also know how far he needs to cast by his knowledge of the river. For those who have not reached this stage of competence, it is as well to make two or three casts onto a smooth part of the river into any available lane of reflected light, but away from the fish, watching all the time for the small ring on the water where the fly has plopped down. Other than on the darkest nights this fly entrance is visible, and is very clear indeed under the moon. I shall have more to say about the moon later, but it is no bad scheme to take out a

122 *To find the line in the dark. Note light colour of fly-line.*

person by moonlight if he or she has not fished before at night.

I don't much like the idea of judging distance by tying pieces of cotton on the line at intervals to mark 10 or 15 yd outside the rod tip. The cotton may come undone, or the wrong mark may be felt. In some places where distance is a critical matter it is sensible to go to the place at which you will stand during the day and count the number of pulls that are required to strip line from the reel to reach the desired lie; the same number may then be withdrawn in the dark. On the whole though it is best to rely on the feel of the rod to judge the length of line you are casting.

The cast must alight delicately on the water. Sea trout will not tolerate splashy casts. It helps if aim is taken at the far bank; the line will then straighten in the air parallel to the water surface before gently falling. Do not cast at the water because the line will hit the river under power. Other than in rough water over stickles, avoid making roll casts because

they create more surface disturbance than a carefully-executed overhead cast.

It is as well when fishing in the dark to check every 15 minutes that all is well with the fly and leader. It is quite possible, even with a single-hooked fly, for the nylon to take a turn about the body, resulting in a fly pulled sideways on the retrieve. With a treble-hooked tube the nylon sometimes becomes jammed between the three hooks of the treble. Much time may be wasted fishing on in ignorance of the fly's condition. To check, reel in the line, or let loose line drift away downstream if wading; hold the rod in the centre of its length with one hand and run the other hand along to the tip and down the line/leader to the fly. This method is illustrated in figure 122, and is better than holding the rod vertically up in the air with one hand whilst groping for the invisible line with the other — almost without fail the leader will wrap itself around the rod and line guides.

The weather and the water

Sea trout are not caught by your staying at home. All the same, there are occasions when chances may be judged in advance to be slim for the night to come, and others when activity may be expected. The peak of the sea trout season is from the end of June to the middle of September. Before this period there will be few fish in from the sea, for the shoals of schoolies have not yet arrived. You will, however, have a bonanza if you are lucky enough to hit an early passing group of 2-pounders as May runs into June and a number of fish of this size make their way up river in company with each other. Such good

fortune may be yours only once in a couple of years, but early June is the time, and by an hour after midnight you may have three or four fish of $2\frac{1}{2}$, 3 or even 4 lbs on the bank. They will be in lovely condition. The nights grow cold as the September equinox approaches; the pleasure of fishing lessens in the longer darkness of the nights that may be chilled by the gales that tend to arise at that time of year. Sea trout fishing falls off in such conditions. September fish are darker than the earlier arrivals, their bellies may be swollen with roe, the flesh soft, pale and not worth eating or freezing. How should you judge your chances in advance and decide whether to fish or go to bed?

Air and water temperatures relative to each other, as in early season salmon fishing, and water levels, are, unsurprisingly, the clues to peal behaviour. Also the tide and the moon play their parts. Spring tides may bring in fresh fish, particularly if there is a freshet at the same time. Warm still cloudy nights are best, the clouds acting as a blanket over the river to keep the air warm. The atmosphere does not have to be warmer than the water, but if the water is markedly warmer than the air, chances are not good. When you have been wading for half an hour put your hand down into the river — if it feels as warm as milk still frothing in the bucket of the hand milker, then it is too warm! The air cools much more rapidly after dark if there is no cloud. Thus the starlit night is suspect as the atmosphere may chill rapidly; even so, on starlit nights good sport may be expected if there is a warm and gentle breeze. Cold winds are not good — if your hands chill rapidly when casting do not expect many sea trout. Don't be put off going to the river if it is windy two hours before dusk in the summer — winds usually fade away as the light fails.

Most anglers do not like the moon. How often do you hear 'I suppose the moon will be up soon and spoil it all'. Take no notice. Go fishing, but with great stealth and care. If the moon rises an hour or so after dusk, lifting over the trees to the east, I carry on. Some of my best nights have been in moonlight, and I can see no reason why you should not be successful, provided you are particularly careful to cast delicately and move with the greatest possible stealth. The position of the moon must be taken into account: no angler should allow himself to be silhouetted with the moon behind him. If you must fish with the moon to your back, keep below the river bank, or try to fish with a background of trees. A moon that shines up the river is very much better than one that shines down stream — just as is the case with the sun and a south to north flowing salmon river at midday. If you fish facing the moon you'll be all right; you'll be able to fish with great accuracy, see each dimple on the water, and pitch the fly exactly where desired at a fish you have marked. I recall two nights in early September 1979, fishing with two brothers in moonlight so bright that we had no difficulty in seeing each other when wading many yards apart.

5 September. Top of Embankment Pool. David and self three sea trout. Tail of the Manse, Charles two sea trout of 3 lb 6 oz. and 12 oz. All between 9 pm and midnight on 1 in. Alexandra tubes. Total 7 lb 14 oz.

and

123 *David and Charles, 7 September: three brownies and nine school peal.*

7 September. Same pools. Same rods. Nine sea trout, three browns. Total over 12 lb. 1 in. Alexandra and Silver Stoat's Tail tubes. All quiet from dusk at 9 pm until 11.30 pm, then took fish by 1.30 am.

The second night was instructive. Don't give up if fish fail to come on the take at the most likely time after dusk — these schoolies came to life two hours later than the previous night, 48 hours before. We were fishing a single bank; on the opposite side of the river were three members of the opposition who went home too soon and never knew what they had missed. You never know with sea trout!

Sub-surface lures

It is as well to arrive at the river at least half an hour before dusk, put on the midge repellent and then tackle up at once whilst there is still sufficient light to knot on the fly and attach the leader. If using one of the two suggested tube flies you will tie on the treble with the tucked half blood; if your choice is an eyed fly then use the Turle knot. In both cases ensure that the nylon is not stretched when tightening the knot — stretched nylon will not straighten, and an inch or so of slightly curly leader in front of the fly is likely to be visible to a cautious fish. Stretching may be avoided: in the tucked half blood draw

gently on the end to be cut off, rather than on the main leader which will not be stretched. In the Turle do not excessively tighten the knot of two turns made on the main leader to form the loop through which the hook is passed. In both cases moisten the knot in your mouth before drawing up tight.

Next wipe down the leader with sink mix and then, with the rod on the bank or a rock, let out the fly and leader into the river to soak. If the leader streams out in the current, with just a yard or two of line outside the rod tip, this will wash off any Fuller's Earth which might otherwise colour the leader light grey on the first two or three casts, and the

124 *Lara Bingham netting a peal.*

125 *Reporting the catch on CB radio.*

126 *Another peal caught.*

127 *Two school peal, which migrated to sea earlier in the season, and came back for Peter Moskovitz.*

nylon will soften and straighten. When you start to fish, the first few casts must sink at once under the surface. They will not do this if these precautions have not been taken, the leader will stand out on top of the water film, each knot joining the tapered sections will make a small wake, and the peal will not accept your fly.

Now sit on the bank to watch and wait. There is much to be learned if you sit still for a while: peal will be revealed as they jump and splash at dusk. There is also much to be appreciated in the half hour transition from day to night: keep still to watch the carrion crows slide down silently from the sky to roost in fir trees; the duck flight speeding up the river — duck fly with purpose and do not idle; tawny owls grumble a little as they wake up and prepare to shiver the mice with their first full call; bats come out to hawk the insects of the night. In Ireland they say you must see three bats before starting to fish; perhaps an Irishman can tell one bat from the next, as this is beyond me I wait until I can no longer distinguish individual heads of cow parsley, and the rocks of the far bank blend to make a dark mass. It is better to start 15 minutes after you might have safely commenced casting than to scare the fish by opening too soon.

Pick up the rod, draw a few pulls off the reel and make your first cast almost downstream; then at 45° downstream; and then straight out; then 45° upriver. Pull off another 6 in. and go through the same arc again. It is best to make the first cast downstream; if made upriver the line may cover peal before the fly. Gradually lengthen the cast and then start to work your way down the pool, either shuffling along under the

bank or wading forward a foot at a time. If casting down and across keep the rod point close to the water and pointing at the fly; the line should be over the forefinger of your rod hand and held in the fingers of the free hand, which will be sensitive to those tiny plucks and tweaks of the interested fish.

With the rod pointing down the line directly at the fly the smallest interference with its progress will register with the angler. Of course not all the plucks will be sea trout, some will be made by brown trout; finding out which is one of the surprises of the night! There is little need to retrieve much line when casting down and across — just a yard or two which may be shot on the next cast. Keeping the rod point close to the water surface has one adverse result in the 45° down and across throw — the belly of the line may swing over the river too fast. There are only two ways in which the speed of travel may be cut down: wade out further or mend over the line. On the whole I would suggest it is better to wade out another yard than to make any disturbance by mending the line in the glassy stillness of a well-populated pool tail.

The throw made up and across hooks fish more securely than down-river casting. This is also true when comparing the results of fly fishing by day for wild brown trout — the wet fly cast down does not hook as securely as the upstream wet, or the imitative dry, which seems to me to produce the heavier, as well as the more soundly-hooked trout. If the results of casting up or down in sea trout fishing were carefully analysed on an individual fish-weight basis I believe the figures would show that heavier fish come from the upstream throw. This is not irrational, for the fly coming back with the current, even though retrieved at a slightly faster rate than the flow, will still fish deeper than the fly lifted close to the surface by the current as it swings across the river or hangs downstream of the angler. Remember, heavy fish tend to inhabit the deeper lies. If the angler is in the tail of a pool the river will have greater depth above his stand. The upstream cast also hooks more firmly because the fly is drawn back into the scissors, rather than being pulled out of the mouth if the fish is below the fisherman.

The actual take varies: sometimes the line just stops swinging: there is a soft dead moment as both fish and angler realize that something is different; and then activity breaks loose. Sometimes the take is hard and savage but not visible; this is usual on the upstream cast. A sharp tug and thrashing moonlit spray may pinpoint the sea trout that has taken downstream in shallow water. Previously, I always hung on tight to these fish, fearing they would run out of the tail of the pool, but they don't, and if handled gently the majority swim through the current, pass the angler and make their fight above him until they tire.

After the take raise the rod high to keep as much line out of the water as possible. As I have said, most fish go up, and hard for the far bank; a 2- or 3-pounder may pull off 20 yd of line in his first run, which is terminated by one, two or three leaps. All you can do at this distance is keep the rod high and rely on top quality hooks, nylon and St. Peter. It is no good entering the controversy of whether to keep the rod up or drop the point at this distance; it won't make any difference with so much line off the reel. If a sea trout jumps when on a short line I always drop my point — there is no worry about the nylon strength—that is adequate—but the hook hold is always somewhat suspect with a peal until he is in the net.

It is necessary to accept that a higher percentage of sea trout will come unhooked than salmon. This is because their mouths are softer, particularly those that have arrived recently from the sea. You may attempt to reduce losses by an additional flying treble trailing $\frac{1}{10}$ in. behind the tail of the fly. I have used this method successfully, but there is a disadvantage; the treble may pierce the net meshes and may have to be cut free. If you are in a position where sea trout may be beached, then the additional flying treble has an advantage over the single hook.

There is also a technique to netting at night. It is no good scooping about in the dark in the area where you think the peal is swimming, particularly if you are fishing two flies, for you are bound to catch one in the net and the trout will break free. You must wait until the beaten fish turns on his side on the surface. This moment of revelation will come and is always sudden. Scanning the river to pinpoint his position your eyes then become aware of his flank, which will show as a light grey bar on the dark surface of the river however black the night. Not until this happens should you make a move to scoop him out. Once in the net tuck the handle under your free arm, thrust the rod butt down inside the top of a wader, and sort him out. You have the priest handy on the cord: knock him on the head whilst still in the net; take out the hook; drop him into the bass; hook up the net once more on the dog clip and go for another.

There will come the time when you have a tangle — generally this cannot be sorted out without a light and some repairs on the bank. Wade gently ashore, go 10 or 15 yd into the field, turn your back on the river and then use the torch. When all has been repaired don't forget to wipe the leader with sink mix before carrying on with the fishing — if you don't the natural grease from your hands will transfer to the nylon when you make knots and the leader will not then sink at once.

It is all totally absorbing, going for a sea trout in the dark. I remember fishing the river Laune in County Kerry in the south west corner of Ireland with two friends. We started at about 9.30 pm — the next time I looked at my watch it was midnight, and later it was still

midnight when I took another glance: the watch had stopped. Concentration on the fly as it swam in the stream, the splash of a fish newly arrived in the pool, the tense expectation that the next cast would be the one: all these had no place in time. The setting was the isolated but not lonely world of the night sea trout fisher, who never knows the moment of the next take.

On another occasion the casting rhythm seemed uneven; still thinking about the fish over there in the river I reached up to remove a blob of weed hanging from the fly outlined against the glimmer of the sky — if I didn't shriek I certainly let go of the 'weed' smartly: it was a bat! You will find that bats often touch your fly-line. The moving fly and the line must be picked up on their radar, and it is not unusual for one to be hooked in the skin, not in the mouth, for bats field insects in a flap

128 *The seven peal from Embankment Glide 12 August 1984 on a 9 ft Hardy Farnborough No. 1 carbon fibre fly-rod.*

of skin at the rear of their bodies and then transfer their prey to the mouth.

Don't imagine that half an hour spent on one lie without a touch means there is nothing there. You may fish the same place for an hour and then, suddenly, without warning a fish will strike your fly. He may have been there all the time, or be a new arrival from the next pool down having just skittered over the intermediate stickle. There is no doubt that the best time is the first hour or two after dark. On a warm August night you might start at 9.30 pm, fishing for the sea trout you saw leap up as you waited for the dark, and they usually project themselves vertically out of the river rather than the lunging jump of the heavier salmon. Take 12 August 1984, for example:

Embankment Glide. Self. 10 pm to 12.30 am. Six sea trout opposite the stump in pool tail. One under trees. No. 8 Black Lure. Best fish 2 lb 3 oz. Warm and cloudy.

Seven were enough — too many in fact for the conscience, but if you clean them, pack them carefully in polythene, freeze them and then eat them in December with a bottle of Muscadet you have done the right thing. And then there was the first fish of the season on 22 June — I don't fish at night before the end of that month because there are not many peal about and it tends to be cold after dark.

Lara netted a good sea trout for me 11.15 pm. Right in the channel at the tail of The Manse. No. 8 Black Lure. 3 lb 3 oz.

That fish would not come up into the pool. He stayed and fought downstream in the narrow fast gut. There was nothing to be done. He had made up his mind to stay there, helped by the current in his fight. But Lara crept up behind him and took him tail first with the net — it wasn't cricket really, taking him from behind, but we ate him and he was good. Lara is my youngest daughter and at that time was 16 years old.

Other nights you'll have to wait, the water smoothly gliding by, and not a sign, perhaps until the early hours when one leaps, then another higher up. Put down the coffee, lay aside the half eaten sandwich and fish — you're bound to meet with success.

Surface lures

If your method fails, try another. Give the fat dry fly a swim across the pool. Try Tony Allen's mayfly, the Red Palmer or a bucktail bodied sedge. They all serve the same purpose: to make a V-shaped ripple as they track across the pool. If the peal don't take the floating fly they may still splash at it, just as trout boil at a fly dapped from a boat. At least you know they're there and can try them later with the wet fly.

Some people fish these floating lures only on the darkest nights, saying that is the only way, but I like to see the fly, to anticipate the black snout which breaks the surface and goes away with the lure as the rod tip bends and the butt bucks in your hand. The floating lure is fun, revealing, and heart stopping. Fishing the floating fly is not a tranquil occupation — you need tranquillizers! But, on the whole, this method does not kill as many peal as the sub-surface fly: the Alexandra and the Silver Stoat's Tail.

It isn't always easy to wait for night to fall. We are all impatient. Well, if you must fish, tie on the mayfly and go to the rough stickle at the head of the pool — not the tail, that must be left until it is quite dark. Go instead to the stickle at the top; keep low; cast up and across and let the fly dance back down over the waves whilst retrieving line fast with the left hand. They'll come for it there in the half-light. The peal in the stickles are the small schoolies of about 12 oz., not large, but just as exciting on the take. This is not the 'no drag' presentation of the dry-fly, upstream, chalk-valley man — a bit of drag is enticing to the peal.

Will you be relaxed in the dark or apprehensive of the unknown? The river in the dark is the same river you viewed by day, the inhabitants are the same: the duck, the fox, the snuffling rooting badger, the mink, the owls, the cows, and the sheep in the field behind. The difference is that some that were active by day will now be asleep, whilst others, hidden as they slept down holes or against the trunks of trees, have woken up. The night birds and animals make different noises from those which go about their business in the daylight hours. This can be alarming. Many is the time I've turned around in the river to face the bank and called (with a tremble in the voice) 'Who's there?' There has never been a reply. In the end you become used to the dark. It is a matter of acceptance of the fact, and it is a fact, that no 'ghoulies, and ghosties, and long leggety beasties, and things that go bump in the night' will creep up on you. The Good Lord will not be needed to deliver you from these things.

On the whole it is wise to go with a companion in the first season or two — preferably someone who does not talk too much, but who will share the plea-sure of the midnight break for coffee, a pull from the flask, and join in admiration and discussion of the catch. Such a break is relaxing and severs the tension of the fishing. When you know the river well — each hole and boulder and the stump which trips you up — like the back of your hand, go fishing by yourself but be sure someone has been told where you have gone.

If there is a bit of extra water in the river you must decide whether you wish to fish for salmon by day, or rest and then go out at night for the sea trout. You cannot do both. My own practice is to fish by day for salmon at the start of the spate, just for an hour or two, then again as the spate commences to fall and right on until it has almost run away. After this let the sea trout have your attention — it wouldn't have been much good going for them earlier because the known places you wish to wade would have been too deep. It is no good peal fishing if you are tired. Have a rest in the afternoon, go to sleep and then make your way to the river after a hearty supper — you'll last longer through the night that way and may even fish on to the dawn.

Now there's a thought — the dawn. Sea trout activity builds up in the hour before the light breaks and, when it does, you may find a willing salmon. But it is more tiring to fish in the dark. Even walking over grass fields that look smooth in the afternoon will trip you up at night. There is an extra demand on the senses and muscles to keep upright. This also applies to wading. If you are the least bit unsteady on your feet it is not sensible to wade in the dark — even more so if you do not know the river very well indeed. To fish for three hours may be enough; suddenly you are aware of aching shoulders, and that is a sign to call it a night.

13 Fishing by day

Upstream fly-fishing

It is a dedicated man who fly fishes for sea trout by day in a river in low water, for there are many factors against success. The clarity of the river enables the fish to see him unless he stalks up from below with even greater care than the brown trout man after an old and knowledgeable trout born in the wild. The fineness of the nylon he must use will put the odds on the peal if the hooked fish is of any size — and if he does not use the finest of leaders the sea trout will have nothing to do with him. The odds are on the fish! Most depressing of all is the knowledge that the sea trout are not eating; that there will be no rise however long he waits. And then there is the depth at which they lie — on the bottom.

Peal are not seen by day 'on the fin' watching out for drifting flies. The brown trout, upstream, dry-fly man expects success; if there is going to be a rise, he knows the fly that will hatch, and he may leave the river for a while, returning for the evening rise. Not so the river, sea trout, daylight, fly-fisher. But there is one encouraging factor — he can see the quarry if he wears polaroids. He knows exactly the position of his prey. Of course, spotting the fish without being seen is hard; if you are seen the peal will just melt away — they slide off like grey shadows to the deep parts of the pool, and they don't often come back to allow a second chance.

To pinpoint a fish is the first step. This may entail a crouched approach to peer through the branches of a bankside bush or a clump of cow parsley. To look down from a tree is revealing — but sea trout look up; care must be taken and movement should be slow. What are you looking for? Ideally a single fish should be the target; there are more eyes in a shoal and it only takes one to be alarmed for all the rest to swim away after him. So look for an isolated fish lying in front of a boulder that will mask his downstream view. If he is in shallow water and of a size between 12 and 20 oz. so much the better, for small fish are more responsive. Look carefully at the water for a long time — peal blend well with the grey river bed but their outline will firm up before your eyes, particularly the straight edge of the tail and the shadow on the bottom.

You now have three choices of method on a calm day: the upstream wet fly, the nymph or the small dry fly. It is true that a sea trout lying in deep water will rise to a dry fly, but the action is a rarity. It is more productive to sink your offering down to his level, and for this the copper-bodied nymph is best. The cast must drop the nymph 2 yd above the peal to give it time to sink a couple of feet by the time it drifts by. The fly-line, however, must not enter his window. Use a 12 ft leader, tapering to the finest point, preferably 5X, which is about 3 lb test. Allow the sunk nymph to drift by the fish, recovering line at the same speed as the current, or induce a take by drawing on the line when the nymph is approaching the trout and comes close to his nose. He almost certainly won't take the first time over — in fact you may have to go on casting many times—but there is always the chance the line may slide forward.... The weighted Black & Peacock Spider may be used in the same manner - this gives the peal a second choice, but it does not cut through the water to sink as rapidly as the nymph. To cast up and across in low water by day will produce drag on the line that will frighten the peal — it is better to cast straight up as described.

The small dry fly may be tried, but the response is usually disappointing, for the fish are not close to the surface. If you do see a peal in shallow water, probably the run-off at the tail of a pool will hold one or two, cast your Black Gnat from below to land just behind his head — he then has no chance to inspect, or see the leader, and has to swirl and grab, or lose the chance!

In rough weather a large dry fly may be cast up; or up and across for drag will not matter greatly in the waves. Try the mayfly on a 3X leader. There is no reason why this should not be taken because, other than the leader being in the water, there is little difference between this and dapping from a boat. The leader, however, must not be greased or it will be visible on the surface: even without a greased leader the well-waterproofed, bushy-type of fly will stay afloat.

It is always worth fishing the tail end of a spate using a fly specifically for sea trout during the final hours when there is still a stain of colour in the water. About five years back I was instructing a group of boys at the tail end of a pool in such a condition: it was an area where we would go night-fishing when the river had finally dropped. Lies were being pointed out, bushes to be avoided on the back cast were noted, and the principles of the up and downstream casts made known. At the end of the leader was the No. 8 Black Lure with which those under instruction usually commence night fishing. I cast this up and across then, whilst retrieving over my rod hand forefinger, turned to the group to explain some point. There was a shout from the boys as, behind me, a silver peal flashed up out of the peaty water at the fast-moving fly. We had him next cast and then two more. Sea trout lose caution by day if the water is higher and more coloured than normal.

Upstream spinning

The Mitchell 300 fixed spool reel is supplied with two spools: the shallower of these is ideal for daytime upstream spinning for sea trout. Fill the spool with about 80 yd of 10 lb test nylon monofilament. As to the rod: a light 8 ft 6 in. double-handed salmon spinning rod may be used, but greater pleasure will be experienced with a single-handed rod of 8 ft in length. Either of these should be in fibreglass. An old trout rod may be cut down and fitted with suitable rings and a reel mount 6 or 8 in. above the end button.

A 'BB' ball-bearing swivel should be

tied to the end of the reel line with a tucked half blood. To the other end of the swivel tie on a trace of 1 yd of 8 lb monofilament, and then the spinning bait. Above the 'BB' swivel I used to clip a small fold-over lead to act as a 'stop' to prevent line twist. Such leads may no longer be sold, but Hardy's market an 'anti-kink' ball-bearing swivel incorporating a suspended oval plastic vane; this will not twirl around, and thus does not allow twisting tensions to form in the reel line.

The whole outfit must be light. This particularly applies to the line: if this is of 15 or 20 lb breaking strain the lightweight baits to be used by day for peal will not have sufficient momentum to pull off enough line to make a long cast. At the same time it would be foolish

to expect a trace of less than 8 lb test to give much of a chance with a salmon — and one may take as the bait is worked up the length of a pool.

The bait itself should be small. Try a gold Mepps of size No. 2 or a Long No. 1 in the copper shade. A 1 in. metal Devon minnow is a fair choice — metal is better than wood in these circumstances as some weight is needed if none is present at the line/trace junction.

The fishing is simple enough. Cast up over the shoals, pause a moment to let the bait go down a foot, then spin back in a retrieve that is faster than the current. If the cast is made up and across the return path will be curved, and this is more attractive. Sometimes three or four small sea trout will follow; sooner or later one will have a go unless you are seen as they arrive almost at your feet. Success will not come unless you set about the business crouched and

129 *A daytime peal to the author whilst salmon fishing.*

130 *Lara Bingham into a 'salmon' which...*

131 *turned out to be a 7 lb sea trout.*

almost on your knees. A sea trout hooked in this way may shake itself free. This happens more frequently than with salmon, and may be due to the peal's softer mouth.

Chance encounters when salmon fishing

When spinning for salmon in the spring, and fishing the fly in summer spates, the bait may be taken by a sea trout. The size of the bait or fly may have something to do with the fact that sea trout caught in this manner are usually large. Perhaps peal of under 2 lb are unwilling to go for a bait as large as a 2 in. Devon, and spring, when such a minnow is fished, is not a small sea trout period. Absence of small sea trout does not apply in a summer spate; even so, those peal which take a salmon tube-fly 1 in. long are the larger fish. I have seen a number of sea trout in the 7 and 8 lb class taken by day, but it has not been my good fortune to land one of my own — a few 4-pounders, and even one of over 5 lb, but not a specimen fish.

I was out with Lara salmon fishing on 24 May when a fish took her 1 in. Black Dart. She was casting a short line into the fast neck of a pool when, at about the tenth presentation, she noticed the line/leader junction knot had disappeared down into the white water: raising the rod she found herself attached. The peal weighed 7 lb and took to the air several times before turning on his side when beaten. It was a surprise to see the fish surrender flank-up, a movement associated with the night when the silver bar of a sea trout's side is visible against the black back-ground of the water. Well, they do the same by day.

The preference for large flies by the heavier sea trout is confirmed by the following incidents:

> *4 May 1977. A 4 lb sea trout at 5.15 pm on a No. 1 Hairy Mary in Cattle Drink Pool.*

Fishing for salmon, before the time of arrival of the grilse, I was carrying a tailer with which I pulled him out after a battle in which he spent much of the time under my feet.

> *14 August 1979. Two sea trout of $2\frac{1}{2}$ lb and $5\frac{1}{2}$ lb. The first to Rudolf in Wide Splay and the second, which came three times before making up his mind, in Iron Bars. Both on $1\frac{1}{4}$ in. Copper Dart tubes.*

and

> *18 August 1979. 4 lb sea trout on $1\frac{1}{4}$ in. Copper Dart.*

As a sea trout is a migratory brown trout why should they not have a go as well? They do. Any wild brownie is a specimen fish in an acid moorland river if over the one pound mark. Two have come my way by day on salmon flies.

> *28 April 1979. Saucepan Pool. No. 1 Hairy Mary. A brown trout weighing $2\frac{3}{4}$ lb.*

and

> *19 June 1982. 7.30 am. A brown trout of 1 lb 12 oz. in Cattle Drink on a $1\frac{1}{4}$ in. Black Dart.*

The second brown was the one I ate: pink fleshed and plump it fought well and tasted good. The other brown trout, and the one of the same size taken at night sea trout fishing, were black, hook-jawed cannibals, which, I have no doubt, mistook the flies for small fish.

It is possible to have two strings to your bow in a salmon river where there are also sea trout by adapting your fishing to include the requirements of large peal. Just as you will take salmon from time to time on a dropper when fishing from a boat in a sea trout loch, so also will sea trout be taken in a salmon river by a fly dribbled over the rough surface at the entrance to a pool. This may be done with the single fly at the point of the leader by raising the rod towards the end of the cast, or by using a dropper. The dropper arrangement is the more attractive but entails a greater risk of losing the fish during the subsequent fight if the free fly snags. A long rod will enable the dropper to be dibbled across the surface for a greater distance than a single-handed 10 ft rod. It is a most exciting exercise, watching the small suspended fly trickle over the turbulence of foaming water at the head of a pool — how do they see through all those bubbles? No matter — they do! The point fly during this action is still submerged; out of sight behind the dropper it may well be the fly which is taken. What would you do if two salmon take at once? It has happened, not to me, but I have seen a second salmon follow a hooked fish.

It does not much matter whether the dibbling is done before the pool is fished down for salmon in the conventional manner, in which case the angler starts at the throat, or after the pool has been covered. In neither case will sea trout or salmon be able to see the fisherman through the turbulence where water gushes into the pool. The leader arrangements to fish in such a manner are simple: draw 10 ft of 15 lb nylon from the spool in your pocket, loop it at one end with a blood bight loop for attachment to the fly line, cut through the leader 4 ft below the loop, rejoining the sections with a blood knot of which one end is left protruding by about 4 in. The end which is left long in the blood knot should be the continuation of the top section of the leader — in this way, if the blood knot comes undone for any reason when playing a fish on the dropper, the sea trout or salmon would still be attached. The dropper fly should be tied on with the tucked half blood. Colour choice is not critical to success once the fly is above the surface. More important is a small wake, or trail, achieved with the weight provided by a small double hook. The shrimp fly is my choice, not only for the twin hooks but also the orange colour, which is important under water, where the fly will be during the main length of the retrieve.

There is little difference between the course of action sketched out above; dapping on a loch; and working the dropper from a boat — the same principle is involved in skidding the fly across the water. There is an added attraction in the lure which pierces the surface, being neither in the water nor the sky. Sometimes one dibbles involuntarily in a river when the fly-line is caught and lifted by a strong upstream gust of wind - the airborne line drawns the fly to the surface where it scuttles forward on the waves, sometimes with a pursuing pair of open jaws! Those experiences when a fish follows with body submerged and nose out of the water are moments of helplessness for the angler — he cannot slow down the fly which is in the hands of the wind, neither is he able to speed up the fish. The few seconds of the pursuit are engraved in picture form on the brain, never to be forgotten, together with the thought 'Was it a small salmon or the largest sea trout of my life?'

Boat fishing

Wet fly

The first sea trout I caught of any size was taken on 19 September 1949 from the beat known as Weedy Bay on Loch Maree in Ross. The fish, which weighed 4 lb, fell to either a Black Pennel or a Peter Ross (I forgot to specify which in my diary). We used fine casts of 3x gut on a very bright day with the wind in the west. One would not now fish so weak a nylon, for stronger leaders are available that are less visible. In those years the gut was blue or green in colour, the cast (as it was then called) comprised a number of short sections of reducing diameter joined together. There were many more knots in a gut leader than we would tolerate today.

All casts were soaked overnight in the basin of your hotel bedroom and kept damp whilst fishing between circular wet pads of felt in a cast box of copper or aluminium. If unsoaked gut was used the knots almost invariably broke. The rod was an 11 ft split-cane and on that day I only had one serviceable arm - the other being encased in plaster of paris from fingers to armpit — all the same the fixed right-angled bend at the elbow made a rod support when I played that sea trout with my rod butt tucked into my stomach!

The following two days were blank in an east wind, but 22 and 23 September produced nine sea trout to $5\frac{1}{2}$ lb from Slattadale and the Hotel Beat — but by then one of us had started to dap with

a 16 ft rod, whilst the other continued with the wet fly, which took the heaviest fish on a Black Pennel. In 1950 we tried again, dapping almost exclusively with Blue Zulu, Buck Tail, Loch Ordie and Fore and After flies — these produced 14 sea trout and finnock to $4\frac{1}{2}$ lb in five August days.

Given two reasonably competent anglers the most important contribution to successful fishing from a boat is made by the boatman. It is essential that he knows the water: the shallow banks and loch edges that will produce fish and the deep areas that will not. He will dawdle over the likely banks invisible beneath the waves; he will hurry over the spaces void of fish; he will manoeuvre the boat with skill when a fish is being played and net the catch with practised competence. A good boatman makes the day! Two methods were used on those 1949 and 1950 visits to Scotland: the wet fly and the dap. It is still the same today.

The wet fly-rod should be a long one, 11 ft is better than 10, and carbon fibre is almost essential at that length. Most of the time a floating line will be used, but take a Wet Cel 2 for depth if fish are dour. The leader may be joined to the fly line via the needle knotted collar and should be of the same taper as that described for night fly fishing, reducing from 20 lb at the butt, through 13 lb, to 8 lb at the point, with the addition of a bob fly at the junction of the top two sections. If you are limited to four wet flies for loch sea trout you would be hard put to beat Peter Ross, Mallard & Claret or Black Pennell on the point and a bushy fly such as the Zulu on the bob. These will take both sea trout and salmon.

The longer the rod the greater the

distance you will be able to trickle the bob fly over the surface in the second half of the retrieve as the fly team is drawn to the boat. If a fish comes for the bob take your time before raising the rod, let him go down and then tighten. Ideally I like the boat to be moved slowly up-wind with the two rods (one almost always has a companion) casting out at right angles towards the area of the fish. The flies will then swing around in an arc behind the boat. A curved retrieve is more effective than one made straight in front of the angler and then fished straight back, which is the action if casts are made in front of a down wind drifting boat, but it does favour the rod in the stern. Places should be swapped at lunch time, or every hour. The rod in the bows can even the odds to a limited extent if he makes a longer cast than the man in the stern.

The dap

A dapping rod needs to be between 14 and 18 ft in length. The reel should hold 80–100 yd of 15 lb monofilament joined to 10 yd of floss nylon blow line. The whole is placed over some old fly line to fill the reel drum. The fly will be fished off a 1 yd length of 8 lb monofilament tied to the end of the blow line.

The essential weather contribution is a breeze: if too light the blow line will not billow out ahead; if too strong the fly will be blown off the water.

To fish draw the floss line through the rod rings and allow it to stream out ahead in the wind. The rod tip is then lowered until the fly scuttles across the water. The nylon trace must not touch the surface of the loch — just the fly. The more floss one is able to extend, the further away from the boat the fly may be fished, and the wider the arc covered by swinging the rod tip from side to side. It is an exciting, simple, fascinating method, well-suited to a person who cannot cast far with a wet fly. But skill, or rather control, is required to hook the sea trout which rises unexpectedly from the depths, curves over and goes down — you must wait until the tail has departed below the waves: then set the hook! Do not rely solely on the dap. Take rods in the boat to fish the wet fly as well, not only in conditions which make dapping impossible, but also to rest your eyes from the strain of constantly searching the water head to keep the fly in sight.

The colour of the dapped fly makes little difference: what is required is a bushy lure which will dance on the waves when thoroughly waterproofed with Supafloat. A No. 8 hook is right for the Loch Ordie, a bucktail monstrosity of your own design or the natural mayfly favoured in the west of Ireland. If none of these succeed, go ashore and catch a brace of grasshoppers!

14 The torn gill flap

A sea trout story

The grey-muzzled, black labrador dog lay on the damp heather. His back was pressed against the circular growth rings at the end of one of the two cut tree trunks that, together with transverse planks, spanned the stream to form a foot bridge. He was content to lie there warmed by the sun of an early December day, which had melted the white frost from the ground. He was not alone. He could touch with his black nose the soles of a pair of smooth-studded, cracked, leather boots, which protruded, toes down, from under a gorse bush. The boots belonged to his owner who was also old, worn smooth by life, and whose face was cracked and crinkled like the boots. The dog accepted the fact that his leader lay under the bush because he had been before to the place where the old man did this thing: it was enough for the dog to guard his master's back. He must not go to the owner of the boots to assure him of his presence or he would be chided — his instruction was to 'lie there' and this he did.

The boots had been still for a long time; the arthritic knees above were damp; the stomach was flat on the ground and the back arched upwards, propped there by wet elbows; the chin, cupped in the supporting hands, was cold; the eyes, through polaroid spec-tacles, cut through the water surface film into the stream. They were fixed on a pair of spawning sea trout whose tails waved over small stones and golden gravel. The cock fish was large for a peal, all of 5 lb thought the old man, and he attended a smaller hen whose silver flank shone momentarily as she arched her spine twice in an egg extruding spasm. The cock fish saw the convulsion, and the aroma of the eggs being carried into the gravel crevices by the current stimulated his purpose: moving up, he lay alongside the female, overlapping her in length at head and tail, and with a quiver his curved body expelled the fertilizing milt. The mating had been consumated many times, and after each tender, exhausting expulsion he dropped back two feet to guard the redd whilst both recovered strength. Sometimes the hen left him, swimming away out of sight of the watcher, but the cock remained.

The male fish was not worn and diseased, as were the cock salmon spawning in the stream, but the red of his gill rakes was exposed by a torn gill flap on the side nearest to the old man. The fish had been born in the stream five years before: had left as a two-year-old fingerling in spring for the sea where it had fed for five months before return-ing later that year to fertilize, by chance of proximity, the eggs of a hen four times his weight. He had returned to the sea after Christmas and further coastal feeding had lifted his weight to twenty ounces on his second spawning run.

On both of these visits he escaped the estuary salmon and mullet nets, for his slim body slipped through the nylon mesh, but the second encounter stripped scales in a dark rash from his silver flank. At the end of the third marine regeneration he swam high in the water along the coast to the estuary of the river of his birth, entered the fresh water and ran upstream for 5 miles: there a poacher's gill net caught him. He did not drown, as had salmon trapped before him with their heads stuck in the mesh, for his head became jammed up to the gills a few moments before the net was drawn to the bank. The poacher grabbed the fish by the tail and in the twisting struggle a gill cover had been torn. He escaped, the wound healed, but the shortened flap no longer covered the blood laden rakes that took oxygen from the water. The fish was marked for life.

The old man knew nothing of these adventures but he recognized the damaged fish as one he had seen in other places in the stream over the past two weeks, several redds having been dug by the couple whose spawning was near completion. The toes of the boots drew at the heather roots; the elbows pushed back; the old man backed out of the hole in the gorse bush and sat on his haunches, slowly straightening his back. The movement was painful. The dog rose to rub his muzzle on the extended hand before both walked home to the stone cottage set under the hill beneath the gnarled wind-blackened beech trees of the moor.

They lived in simplicity, man and dog; no carpet warmed the slate flags of the floor; no cloth covered the pine table; and the dog's place was a basket of rush worked by a blind man in the distant town. But the cottage welcomed them as it had others within the protection of its walls over the centuries. A black cast-iron range gave out heat to a Windsor chair close to a pile of logs, and on the table stood an oil lamp beside the old man's spectacles. When he had left his house in the town, after the death of his wife, he had thought at first to install an electric generator, but the disruption of such an event put him off, and whilst considering the matter he had made do with oil lamps. In the end he bought a Tilley, by the bright light of which he tied his trout and sea trout flies — otherwise he used the lamps which were silent and gave out a warming glow. The range was set back in a fireplace surmounted by a granite slab on which were a badgers skull, a pair of binoculars, and a jar of spills to light the lamps. Above the mantlepiece hung an oil painting of a woman fishing a moorland stream. A row of fishing rods hung from nails driven into a strip of wood along one wall, a line dryer from the bygone age of silk rested on top of a dresser by some plates, and a trout net was propped against the wall. Books, large and small, leather-bound and cloth-covered, together with a portable wireless were on the table. The plastered walls were relieved by water-colours of birds — snipe, duck, geese and an oil of curlews flighting at dawn to estuary sand bars uncovered by the tide. The old man looked about and took comfort from his things.

He fed the dog. Ladling biscuit with a tin mug from a paper sack into a milk churn lid he added half a tin of meat and a soaking of milk from the can he collected daily from the farm. The dog ate to one side of the room whilst the old man warmed his knees before the opened door of the stove which glowed behind the bars. Later he also ate: a meal of a pigeon he had shot flighting in to roost earlier in the week, a baked potato which had cooked during his absence and some sprouts - all washed down by a glass of red wine from the town, which he visited on pension day, driving there in a battered Land Rover with the dog on a sack in the back.

After his meal he carried the dishes through into the scullery, worked the handle of the pump which drew water from the well and washed up, warming the cold water with a dousing from the kettle on the range. Settling himself in the chair, the wine to hand, he turned on the news and then reached over and tapped the barometer. Rain would come he thought, out of the west, for a wind was moving over the moor and the clouds had lowered as he walked home. He turned off the wireless and reached for a book as the patter of the first drops touched the windows. For a while he read until his chin fell forward and he slept. Later, in the darkness of the bedroom, he heard the drumming of the rainstorm on the roof.

The level rose rapidly in the stream as the rain ran from the hills; the flow coloured, white froth formed in the pockets under the peat banks and the last of the autumn leaves from the beech trees were carried away downstream. The sea trout with the damaged gill went with them. Slipping out of the stream into the river he worked his way down the valley, pool by pool, over the weirs and through the salmon ladders until he reached the gentler waters winding through the lowland farms. He came

at last to the weir that divided the river from the salt waters of the sea. He was of the river and of the sea: the one his nursery, the other healed his spawning sores and gave him food. The sea accepted him, absorbing without acknowledgement the return of its foster child from the river that gave the fishes birth. For nine months he swam and fed in the ocean paths. His pale, softened flesh deepened in colour, his flanks hardened, his muscles were tuned for an August river entry as he swung north up the estuary that had welcomed him before. He settled below the weir in company with three grilse and several smaller peal that made their way upstream in the night. For seven days and nights he waited with the grilse, pestered by the hooks and leads of small boys who cast worms into the pool. In the second week thunder rolled over the moor, lightning cut the sky and grey sheets of rain drifted down to fill the runnels, the brooks, the upland river — and then the water rose over the weir. Momentarily he was visible as he leaped and then he was swallowed by the dark water above the sill.

The old man had fished for trout in the summer. Watched by the dog he cast his Wickham's Fancy up ahead and struck sharply when a brownie dimpled at the fly. Small as they were he ate the trout and the magpies picked over the skins and heads he scraped off the plate onto the garden wall. He no longer fished for salmon — there was no point for he could not eat so large a fish and there was no need to sell. But sea trout, particularly the small ones — they were a different matter. He loved a sea trout. He sat at the table in his cottage as the rain came down: in front of him was a fly-tying vice with a No. 8 hook in the jaws. The old man looked at the hook, which he had placed there by habit, forming in his mind the kind of fly he would make to suit the water when he fished in two nights time. The spate in the river would have run away by then, but a little colour would remain and there would be fresh peal in the tails of the pools. A large fly? Yes, he ought to dress an offering of substance to match the stained water. He removed the No. 8 and clamped tight on a No. 4. The dressing was plain: a silver body, a teal wing and black varnish for the head. He tied another — just in case he lost the first. They were good flies with no fancy trimmings — he stroked their points on the flat of an oil stone and tested them on the nail of his thumb.

Two evenings later he sat on a stone by the river, waiting for the light to fade. The chosen pool darkened in front of him, bats jiggered over the surface as they hawked for flies, and a rabbit, caught by a stoat, squealed on the far bank. All became quiet. The dog also watched the water and tested the wind of night. They had seen peal jump, and a salmon had leaped once to bash down with a crash which sent waves lapping under the bank beneath their feet. A lightening to the east gave notice of a moon. The old man rose; the time had come. He picked up the rod, retrieved the fly and leader from the pool where they had been soaking, and drawing line from the reel cast out towards the break in the smooth water where the glide ran out into the stickle below. On the third cast the line straightened, there was a flurry of white spray in the shallows as a small peal took the fly. The short fight was followed by surrender — he drew the fish across the surface and beached it on the shingle at his feet. He tapped the one-pound sea trout on the head, removed the hook and tossed the fish to the dog, which carried it to the stone where he had left his bag.

The moon rose above the hill, shining directly into his eyes and in reflection from a path of brightness on the water. He waded out to cast square across into the avenue of light, the fly pitched in and was taken within two yards in the deep water below the bushes on the opposite bank. For a moment all was still, his hands felt for information, his eyes searched for the line, which moved with increasing speed to the head of the pool where a sea trout leaped twice with awesome crashes — then all went slack. The old man stripped in fast, drawing the yards in over his finger, his heart sank and then, below him, the water bulged as the sea trout turned, then moved up level with his legs. The dog came to the shingle bank as the old man backed out of the water when the sea trout showed a silver side. The beaching was gentle, a push from behind and there he lay on his side, the damaged gill flap visible in the light of the harvest moon.

The old man removed the hook, wet his hands, turned the fish to the river of nativity and slid him away. The sea trout wallowed, righted itself and faded from sight with a stroke of the square tail. The old man, who could not eat so large a fish, lifted his hat an inch and murmured 'We'll meet again, by the foot bridge, in December.'

Bibliography

Chaytor, A.H. *Letters to a salmon fisher's sons.* First published 1910. Reprinted 1983, André Deutsch.

Crow, S.H., Lt Col. *Hampshire Avon salmon.* First published 1966, E.M.A.P. Ltd, Oundle Road, Peterborough.

Falkus, Hugh. *Sea trout fishing.* First published 1975, Witherby.

Falkus, Hugh. *Salmon fishing.* First published 1984, Witherby.

Gray, L.R.N. *Torridge fishery.* 1957. Nicholas Kaye Ltd.

Orton, D.A. (ed.) *Where to fish.* Published every other year by *The Field.*

Scott, Jock. *Greased line fishing.* Seeley Service. Undated, but probably compiled just before 1939. It is about Arthur Wood, who was one of the originators of floating line salmon fly fishing.

Voss-Bark, A. (ed.) *West Country fly fishing.* B.T. Batsford Ltd, 1983.

Suppliers

Fishing tackle may be obtained from many stockists. It is suggested that the following manufacturers and wholesalers will provide information on your nearest specialized retail source if they do not supply direct.

Rods

Bruce & Walker Ltd, Huntingdon Road, Upwood, Cambridge
Fosters of Ashbourne, 32, St John Street, Ashbourne, Derbyshire
Hardy Bros (Alnwick) Ltd, Willowburn, Alnwick, Northumberland
Partridge of Redditch Ltd, Mount Pleasant, Redditch, Worcestershire
Pegley-Davies Ltd, Hersham Trading Estate, Walton-on-Thames, Surrey
Taylor & Johnson Ltd, 19, Broadground Road, Lakeside, Redditch, Worcestershire

Reels

Bruce & Walker Ltd
Hardy Bros (Alnwick) Ltd
Leeda Tackle, 14–24, Cannon Street, Southampton
Pegley-Davies Ltd
Taylor & Johnson Ltd

Gye nets

Taylor & Johnson Ltd

Nets

Hardy Bros (Alnwick) Ltd
Pegley-Davies Ltd
Taylor & Johnson Ltd

Flies and fly lines

Hardy Bros. (Alnwick) Ltd
Pegley-Davies Ltd
Taylor & Johnson Ltd

Fly-tying materials

E. Veniard Ltd, 138, Northwood Road, Thornton Heath, Surrey

Fish hooks

Partridge of Redditch Ltd
Dutton Campbell Dixon & Co, Duck Lane, Maids Moreton, Buckingham

Polaroid spectacles

Pegley-Davies Ltd
Taylor & Johnson Ltd
Multisport Optical, 9, Ham Lane, Powick, Worcester

Fly boxes

Richard Wheatley & Son Ltd, Century Works, Walsall

Jungle cock feathers

Fisherman's Feathers Ltd, Manor Mill, Crowan, Nr Camborne, Cornwall

Waders

Pegley-Davies Ltd
Taylor & Johnson Ltd

Spey Devon minnows

Fog Fishing Tackle, Ross-on-Wye, Herefordshire

Index